RUBAIYAT OF OMAR KHAYYAM
BIRD PARLIAMENT

Rubaiyat of Omar Khayyam
Bird Parliament

Farrid ud-Din Attar

translated by EDWARD FITZGERALD

Selected and edited by Tony Briggs

PHOENIX

A PHOENIX HARDBACK

This hardback edition first published in Great Britain in 2009
by Phoenix,
an imprint of Orion Books Ltd,
Orion House, 5 Upper St Martin's Lane,
London WC2H 9EA

1 3 5 7 9 10 8 6 4 2

Copyright © Orion Books Ltd 2009

A CIP catalogue record for this book
is available from the British Library.

ISBN 978–0–7538–2678–2
Typeset by Deltatype Ltd, Birkenhead, Wirral
Printed and bound in Great Britain by
Clays Ltd, St Ives plc

The Orion Publishing Group's policy is to use papers that
are natural, renewable and recyclable products and
made from wood grown in sustainable forests. The logging
and manufacturing processes are expected to conform to
the environmental regulations of the country of origin.

www.orionbooks.co.uk

Contents

Note on the Authors and Editor

EDWARD FITZGERALD was born on 31 March 1809, the son of John and Mary Purcell. FitzGerald was his mother's maiden name, assumed by the family when she received a large inheritance. Educated at King Edward VI School, Bury St Edmunds, and Trinity College, Cambridge, he graduated in 1830 after befriending Thackeray and getting to know Tennyson. Most of his subsequent life was spent in or near Woodbridge, Suffolk. He travelled little and took up no profession. His first venture into print was a short biography of Bernard Barton, a Quaker poet, following his death in 1849. Seven years later FitzGerald married Barton's daughter, Lucy; the couple soon separated. Among his many close male friends the most important was the orientalist Edward Cowell, who first introduced him to the Persian language and literature. The first edition of the *Rubaiyat of Omar Khayyam* was published anonymously in 1859, almost failed but was discovered and promoted by the editor of the *Saturday Review* and the Pre-Raphaelites. Among FitzGerald's other published works were translations from Aeschylus, Sophocles, Calderon and Jami. In 1864 he befriended a Lowestoft fisherman, Posh Fletcher; the two became partners in herring-fishing, and their unusual relationship lasted for more than a decade. On 14 June 1883 FitzGerald died in Norfolk, leaving behind a voluminous series of letters which reveal a man of great culture, insight and humour. A monument to his artistic sensitivity, they also sum up the uneventful life of vicarious pleasure enjoyed by a modest, reclusive literary genius.

OMAR KHAYYAM, whose second name means 'tent-maker', was a Persian astronomer, mathematician and freethinker whose dates have been reasonably well established as 1048–1131. All his life was spent in his native town of Naishapur, where his most celebrated achievement was to direct a commission charged with reforming the calendar, which was done with remark-able accuracy. This brought him celebrity in the Islamic world, but he was not known for his poetry until several decades after his death, when the now famous *Rubaiyat* (or *rubais*, quatrains) began to be ascribed to him with varying degrees of authenticity. His beliefs are difficult to determine with accuracy but the overall impression gained from the quatrains is compounded of rationalism, light cynicism and a hedonistic spirit. His reputation as a poet, more substantial in the West than in Persia itself, was popularised by FitzGerald's adaptations.

FARRID UD-DIN ATTAR was born about a decade after the death of Omar Khayyam and lived until c. 1230. Originally a druggist, Attar renounced the world in order to lead a life of stern asceticism, and became a prolific writer of Sufic works. His most valuable achievements were a biographical study of eminent mystic divines and instructional writings known as *mathnawis*, including the *Pandnama* (*Book of Counsels*) and the *Mantik ut-Tair* (*Speeches of the Birds*).

TONY BRIGGS, Emeritus Professor of Russian at Birmingham, Senior Research Fellow at Bristol University, is a well-known writer and broadcaster on Russian cultural affairs and European poetry. His recent translation of *War and Peace* was critically acclaimed. Among his many publications are six editions in the Everyman's Poetry series.

Chronology of FitzGerald's Life

Year	Age	Life
1809		31 March: Edward Purcell born at the White House, Bredfield, Suffolk, the seventh child of Mary (*née* FitzGerald) and John Purcell
1816	7	Purcell family moves to France. Two years at Saint-Germain-en-Laye and then Paris
1818	9	Mrs Purcell's father dies, leaving her a fortune; the family assumes the name of FitzGerald and returns to England
1821	12	FitzGerald sent to King Edward VI School, Bury St Edmunds. Lifelong friendships formed with William Bodham Donne and James Spedding
1824	15	Family moves to Wherstone Lodge, near Ipswich
1826	17	Enters Trinity College, Cambridge. Lifelong friendships formed with John Allen, W. H. Thompson and Thackeray

Chronology of his Times

Year	Literary Context	Historical Events
1812	Dickens born	Napoleon enters Russia
		America declares war on Britain
1813	Jane Austen, *Pride and Prejudice*	East India Company monopoly abolished
		Wellington invades France
1814	Wordsworth, *The Excursion*	Napoleon deposed, banished to Elba
1815		Defeat of Napoleon at Waterloo
		Congress of Vienna
		Corn Laws passed
1820	Shelley, *Prometheus Unbound*	Accession of George IV
1821	Death of Keats	Death of Napoleon
	Births of Baudelaire, Dostoyevsky, Flaubert	
1822	Birth of Matthew Arnold	Famine in Ireland
	Death of Shelley	Greek Declaration of Independence
1824	Death of Byron	
1827	John Clare, *Shepherd's Calendar*	

Year	Age	Life
1830	21	Graduates, and pays a brief visit to Paris with Thackeray
1833	24	Befriends William Kenworthy Browne: close relationship for twenty years
1835	26	FitzGerald family moves to Boulge Hall, Woodbridge, Suffolk
1837	28	Settles in Boulge Cottage
1842	33	15 September: first meeting with Carlyle
1844	35	Collects historical research materials for Carlyle
1846	37	Working on *Euphranor, A Dialogue on Youth*

Year	Literary Context	Historical Events
1829		Catholic emancipation
1830	Tennyson, *Poems, Chiefly Lyrical*	Accession of William IV
1832	Death of Scott	First Parliamentary Reform Act
1833	Carlyle, *Sartor Resartus*	Abolition of slavery in British Empire
1834	Death of Coleridge	Trials of Tolpuddle Martyrs
		New Poor Law establishes workhouses
1837	Dickens, *Oliver Twist*	Accession of Queen Victoria
1838	Dickens, *Nicholas Nickleby*	Anti-Corn Law League established
1840	Dickens, *Old Curiosity Shop*	
1841	Carlyle, *On Heroes and Hero-Worship*	Robert Peel becomes prime minister
1842	Tennyson, *Poems*	Chartist riots
1843	Death of Southey	
	Wordsworth becomes Poet Laureate	
1844	Elizabeth Barrett Browning, *Poems*	
1845		Famine in Ireland (1845–51)
1846		Repeal of Corn Laws
1847	Charlotte Brontë, *Jane Eyre*	
	Emily Brontë, *Wuthering Heights*	
1848	Thackeray, *Vanity Fair*	Revolutions in Europe
	Formation of the Pre-Raphaelite Brotherhood	

Year	Age	Life
1849	40	19 February: death of Bernard Barton, Quaker friend and poet. Edits and introduces a selection of his work, including biography
1851	42	*Euphranor* published
1852	43	*Polonius: A Collection of Wise Saws and Modern Instances* published
1853	44	Publication of *Six Dramas from Calderon, freely translated by Edward FitzGerald.* Translating Sadi
1855	46	August: Carlyle stays with FitzGerald at Farlingay, near Woodbridge
1856	47	*Salaman and Absal* published. Reads the *Rubaiyat* of Omar Khayyam, which Edward Cowell has discovered in Oxford
		4 November: marries Lucy Barton in Chichester
1857	48	Separates from his wife, and translates many of the *Rubaiyat*
1859	50	9 April: FitzGerald's translation of the *Rubaiyat*, published by Bernard Quaritch
1860	51	Moves to lodgings in Market Hill, Woodbridge

Year	Literary Context	Historical Events
1849	Ruskin, *Seven Lamps of Architecture*	
1850	Wordsworth, *The Prelude* Death of Wordsworth Tennyson, *In Memoriam* Tennyson becomes Poet Laureate	
1851	Ruskin, *Stones of Venice*	Great Exhibition
1852	Thackeray, *Henry Esmond*	Fall of French Republic
1853	Mathew Arnold, *Poems*	
1854	Dickens, *Hard Times* Matthew Arnold, *Poems, Second Series*	Crimean War begins Palmerston becomes prime minister
1855	Tennyson, *Maude, and Other Poems*	
1856	Thomas Hughes, *Tom Brown's Schooldays*	Peace of Paris
1857	Trollope, *Barchester Towers* Elizabeth Barrett Browning, *Aurora Leigh*	Indian Mutiny
1858	George Eliot, *Scenes of Clerical Life*	British Crown assumes control of India
1859	Darwin, *Origin of Species* Tennyson, *Idylls of the King*	Construction of Suez Canal begins
1860	George Eliot, *The Mill on the Floss* Wilkie Collins, *The Woman in White*	

Year	Age	Life
1861	52	Quaritch remainders the translations, offering them for a penny. They are discovered by the editor of the *Saturday Review*, and then by the Pre-Raphaelites
1864	55	Buys a cottage on the outskirts of Woodbridge; has it enlarged, but continues to live in Market Hill. Meets Joseph (Posh) Fletcher
1867	58	The lugger *Meum and Tuum* is built. FitzGerald and Posh form a herring-fishing partnership
1868	59	Enlarged edition of the *Rubaiyat*
1870	61	Partnership with Posh Fletcher dissolved
1872	63	Third edition of the *Rubaiyat*
1873	64	Evicted from his rooms in Market Hill
1874	65	Moves to his 'château', Grange Farm, later known as Little Grange
1876	67	Formally acknowledged as the translator of the *Rubaiyat*. He publishes 'an impudent version of the *Agamemnon*'

Year	Literary Context	Historical Events
1861	J. S. Mill, *Utilitarianism*	Death of Prince Albert
	Death of Elizabeth	American Civil War (−1865)
	Barrett Browning	Victor Emmanuel King of Italy
1862	Christina Rossetti,	
	Goblin Market and	
	Other Poems	
1863	Death of Thackeray	
1864	Trollope, *Can You*	Death of Landor
	Forgive Her?	
1865	Yeats born	
	Kipling born	
	Arnold, *Essays in*	
	Criticism	
1866	Swinburne, *Poems and*	Last cholera epidemic in Britain
	Ballads	
1867	Water Bagehot, *English*	Second Parliamentary Reform
	Constitution	Act
1868	William Morris, *Earthly*	Gladstone becomes prime
	Paradise	minister
	Browning, *The Ring and*	
	the Book	
1869	Matthew Arnold,	
	Culture and Anarchy	
1870	Death of Dickens	Franco-Prussian War
	D. G. Rossetti, *Poems*	Unification of Germany
1871	Darwin, *Descent of Man*	Paris commune
1872	Tennyson, *Gareth and*	Third Parliamentary Reform Act
	Lynette	
	Eliot, *Middlemarch*	
1873	Death of J. S. Mill	Gladstone resigns
1874	Hardy, *Far From the*	Gold Coast annexed
	Madding Crowd	Disraeli prime minister
1876	Mark Twain, *The*	Victoria proclaimed Empress of
	Adventures of Tom	India
	Sawyer	

Year	Age	Life
1879	70	Fourth edition of the *Rubaiyat*
1880–1	71-2	Translations of Sophocles privately distributed
1882	73	*Readings in Crabbe* published by Quaritch
1883	74	14 June: dies at George Crabbe's rectory, Merton, Norfolk;
		19 June: buried in Boulge churchyard

Year	Literary Context	Historical Events
1877	Henry James, *The American*	
1878	Gilbert and Sullivan, *HMS Pinafore* Hardy, *The Return of the Native*	Congress of Berlin
1879	Meredith, *The Egoist*	Zulu War
1880	Deaths of George Eliot and Flaubert	Gladstone's second ministry
1881	Henry James, *Portrait of a Lady*	Death of Disraeli
1882	Virginia Woolf born James Joyce born	British occupation of Egypt
1883	Meredith, *Poems and Lyrics*	Fabian Society founded

Introduction

As to the greatness of the *Rubaiyat*, I know none to be compared with it for power, pathos and beauty in the same line of thought and work, except possibly *Ecclesiastes*

Algernon Swinburne

FitzGerald is to be called 'translator' only in default of a better word. His work is that of a poet inspired by a poet, not a copy . . ., not a translation

Charles Eliot Norton

The scattered colours of the Persian poetry have been changed into a beam of light

F. B. Money-Coutts

FitzGerald . . . stands in his own right as a unique poetical personality

C. M. Bowra

The Omar Industry

Edward FitzGerald is a good friend to English poetry, having lifted it to great and lasting popularity more successfully than anyone else. How has he done this? Let us count the ways.

His long poem, *Rubaiyat of Omar Khayyam*, has broken all literary publishing records (outside the Bible and Shakespeare). As we celebrate the 150th anniversary of this work (published in March 1859) we can thank diligent researchers for the knowledge that it has so far appeared in at least 650 different editions, and a large number of reprints. Half of these have been illustrated, by 150 different artists. One edition measuring 8 millimetres square was the world's smallest book in its day (1900). By contrast, the most lavish version, *The Great Omar*, 'one of the finest examples of the bookbinder's craft', lies at the bottom of the Atlantic, having been unlucky enough to be sent to America on the *Titanic* (1912); a facsimile can be seen in the British Library.

More than a hundred composers have set the *Rubaiyat* to music; the best-known settings range from Liza Lehman's *Evening in a Persian Garden* (1896) to Sir Granville Bantock's vast oratorio, *Omar Khayyam* (1906–09), which calls for two symphony orchestras and a double choir, one of each on either side of the platform. And the poem has had a huge spin-off in countless imitations, tributes, translations into at least *seventy* other languages, parodies and commercial products. FitzGerald's modest little work, which nobody wanted when it was first printed, eventually developed into a veritable industry or cult extending across the world.

This is not to say that the actual poem has been neglected in an orgy of secondary exploitation. On the contrary, no work has been more lovingly enjoyed, committed to memory and singled out for quotation. Only a generation ago all educated people would have instantly recognised stanzas beginning 'Awake, for Morning in the bowl of Night . . .'; 'A Book of Verses underneath the Bough . . .'; 'Myself when young did eagerly frequent . . .'; 'The moving Finger writes, and having writ . . .' or 'Ah, Moon of my Delight who know'st no wane . . .' (For the record, *rubaiyat* is a Persian plural meaning 'quatrains'; the singular form is *rubay*.)

'Wherever the English speech is spoken or read,' an audience was told at the end of the nineteenth century, 'the Rubaiyat have taken their place . . . There is not a hill-post in India, nor a village in England where is not a coterie to whom Omar Khayyam is a familiar friend and a bond of union. In the Eastern states of America his addicts form an esoteric sect. In the cities of the West you will find the Quatrains one of the most thoroughly read books in every club library.' The speaker himself heard them quoted at sunrise 'in one of the most lonely and desolate spots of the high Rockies'. Wherever you went, you could not get away from this poem.

Thomas Hardy loved the work so much that he became a founder member of the Omar Khayyam (Dining) Club in London, and had a stanza from it read to him on his deathbed.

More than half of the entire poem forced itself into the *Oxford Dictionary of Quotations* just be being so well known. Nowadays nobody learns poetry by heart, more's the pity, so this source of folk memory is melting away. It is not without significance that as EFG's (as he often called himself) popularity slowly declines, so apparently does that of poetry itself. (You may have noticed the shrinking poetry sections in our expanding bookshops.)

In bringing out yet another edition of this famous favourite work we have three aims in mind. First, there is a need to present Edward FitzGerald more assertively than before, and establish him as an important English poet rather than merely as a translator and adapter of other men's work. Second, his *Omar Khayyam* quatrains are offered here in an unusual grouping intended to bring out the best qualities of all the first five editions. (This means we are presenting a version designed for readers rather than scholars; see Note on the Texts). Third, we bring to long-overdue prominence another important work of FitzGerald's, *Bird Parliament*, a masterpiece that is still virtually unknown 120 years after its first (obscure) publication.

Edward FitzGerald, unlike many comparable English poets, has not been widely honoured by officialdom, or even properly acknowledged by academics. This seems to be a question of ignorance and neglect more than professorial hostility. Nevertheless, there are doubts about him, and we shall have to confront a number of awkward questions. Was the astonishing popularity of the *Rubaiyat* perhaps based on cheap verses not much better than greetings-card doggerel? Does it matter that they come to us through a form of translation? Is there genuine quality in this work, and what does it consist of? Are there any hidden meanings that might enhance its standing even further? Finally, where should we now locate this writer in the pantheon of English poetry?

The Lives of Two Poets

These questions will not be resolved by looking in detail at the two lives involved, but a little biography may be useful.

Omar Khayyam (1048–1131) is celebrated throughout the Islamic world, but not as a poet. His claim to immortal fame is that he worked as head of a commission of astronomer-mathematicians entrusted with reforming the calendar, whose results proved to be astonishingly accurate – to a single day in 5000 years. Beyond that, most of his life is rather hazy to us, and the composition of his now-famous *rubaiyat* is even more opaque. Although many hundreds of these quatrains have been attributed to him in succeeding centuries, not a single one can be fully authenticated. It is likely that, when they were composed, they were not written down but communicated orally in a manner not far from the way in which some of us, as young men, sang dozens of rude limericks from memory at beer parties. (Tradition has it that a Persian poet of the ninth or tenth century picked up the *rubaiyat* from a boy playing in the street.) Thus it is impossible to determine with any certainty what poems the astronomer actually dashed off in his spare time. Besides which, the quatrains were not grouped in any way. When at last they came to be written down they were gathered in alphabetical order. There is little to be gained by going into this question any more deeply. Most of the ideas in FitzGerald's *Rubaiyat* do have an origin in Persian oral poetry, and many of them may well have been memorably expressed by Omar Khayyam himself, but our attitude towards FitzGerald and his achievement cannot now be governed by an awareness of how accurate he was in translation. Much ink has been used up, a lot of it wasted, in such a pursuit, but today it is surely more important to judge this poetry by its merits in the school of English literature than in the history of translation.

FitzGerald's life story is better documented but quite unremarkable; he enjoyed what he described as a 'talent for dullness'. Born into a wealthy family (31 March 1809), he was educated at King Edward VI Grammar School in Bury St Edmunds, and then at Trinity College, Cambridge, where he met Thackeray, who became his lifelong friend, as did Tennyson, soon afterwards. Without the need to earn a living, EFG entered on a life that had little shape or meaning: a year or two in London, the odd trip to Paris, and then retreat to the Suffolk countryside and coastline where he had been born. From there he barely stirred for the rest of his days, though by the time of his death at the age of seventy-four (14 June 1883) he had exchanged village life for a reclusive existence in the quiet town of Woodbridge.

All the main relationships entered into by EFG were with men. It is clear to us now that, like Tchaikovsky in another country but the same period, he was a homosexual living in an age when this forbidden tendency was not spoken about. Also like the Russian composer, he made the disastrous decision – for compassionate reasons – to marry a lady admirer, and with similarly catastrophic results. Apart from this very brief misalliance he kept humanity at arm's length and lived out a series of contradictions, as a rich man who lived frugally, a gifted individual who lacked enterprise and confidence, a generous man who suffered lifelong feelings of guilt, a serious reader, critic, musician, talented artist and art collector, who was widely regarded, especially in later years, with affection but as an amusing eccentric. He was modest and diffident to a fault, which accounts for the fact that the first five editions of his most famous work omitted his name from the title page, and also that his extensive second-best work (see below) was never published in his lifetime. His self-effacing nature certainly prevented him from developing his considerable poetic powers and writing more.

Of all his close friendships with men, one was particularly decisive. In 1844 EFG befriended a gifted young multilinguist, Edward Cowell, who would one day end up as Professor of Sanskrit at Cambridge. Cowell inspired him to learn other languages and to write. FitzGerald's first published work was *Euphranor* (1851), a kind of Platonic dialogue on the subject of modern education between four undergraduates and a doctor twice their age. This discourse, stylishly written but neither profound nor strongly argued, was best described by its own author as 'a pretty specimen of a chiselled cherry-stone'. It was followed in 1852 by *Polonius: A Collection of Wise Saws and Modern Instances*, a work aptly dismissed by its own preface, which begins, 'Few books are duller than books of Aphorisms and Apophthegms . . .', and then in 1854 by the more successful *Six Dramas of Calderon, Freely Translated by Edward FitzGerald*, in which he struck an attitude towards translation that would become his hallmark. Here and elsewhere (as in his later versions of Aeschylus and Sophocles) he is less concerned with translation as such than with the need to adapt and re-present a foreign text, thus 'making some things readable which others have left unreadable'. Even so, he had not yet found his forte.

It was Cowell who set FitzGerald on his true path by persuading him to learn Persian and read the poets in that language. He mastered this new tongue with some degree of competence, always assisted by Cowell; even when the latter married and took up a post in India the two maintained a long and detailed correspondence. Cowell had come across a fifteenth-century manuscript containing 158 quatrains (*rubaiyat*) ascribed to the eleventh-century poet Omar Khayyam, and he diligently copied them out for his friend to translate. EFG might never have done so, but he plunged into the work with unprecedented powers of application, not least to distract and console himself in the aftermath of his marriage break-up. In 1859 he published his versions of the Persian poet in a thin booklet – 250 copies, seventy-five quatrains taking up twenty-one pages, with a short introduction and a few explanatory notes, price one shilling.

The story of this small publication has become famous. Months ran into years, and it did not sell. Eventually the publisher gave up hope and dumped a few copies into his bargain box, dividing the price of a copy by twelve. (One of those booklets would now cost you thousands of pounds at auction.) It was noticed at last by a young Celtic scholar, Whitley Stokes, brought to the attention of Rossetti and Swinburne, and handed on to Morris, Burne-Jones and Ruskin, who launched it on a dazzling career that would send it round the world in only a few decades and make it the most popular edition of poetry ever published.

The mixed feelings of tremendous admiration for this new work, and mystification, from not knowing who the author was, are nicely caught in a letter addressed to the poet on 2 September 1863 by John Ruskin, though it took ten years to get to him because at first no one knew where to send it:

> My dear and very dear Sir,
> I do not know in the least who you are, but I do with all my soul pray you to find and translate some more of Omar Khayyam for us. I never did – till this day – read anything so glorious, to my mind, as this poem . . . and that, and this, is all I can say about it – More – more – please more – and that I am ever Gratefully and respectfully yours.
> J. Ruskin

This admiration was gradually converted into widespread popularity, promoted by an American critic, Charles Eliot Norton, who took the *Rubaiyat* to the United States, where he gave the volume wide publicity in a very favourable review of 1869. After that the poem never looked back.

The *Rubaiyat of Omar Khayyam*

The important truth behind the amazing triumph of the *Rubaiyat* has still not been asserted with sufficient emphasis or clarity: the success is due far more to

FitzGerald's poetic genius than to Omar as an inspirational force. The first test of this claim is to consult any other translations of the *Rubaiyat*, literal or poetic; many exist, but none of them even approaches FitzGerald's in appeal. Sheer poetic quality, of which we shall see many examples below, is the hallmark of the FitzGerald versions. What is remarkable is the ease with which this elementary principle has been swallowed up in debates about the accuracy of his work as a translator or the possibility that the *Rubaiyat* are meant to be Sufic allegories rather than an open call to hedonism.

Edward FitzGerald's relationship with Omar Khayyam is nothing like that between Chapman and Homer, Dorothy L. Sayers and Dante, or Nabokov and Pushkin. Whatever the literary merits of Omar Khayyam's original writings, FitzGerald set out not to translate but to transform them. 'It is an amusement to me', he wrote, 'to take what Liberties I like with these Persians, who (as I think) are not Poets enough to frighten one from such excursions, and who really do want a little Art to shape them.' (The only Persian poet whom he regarded so highly as to consider him untranslatable was Hafiz.) He set out to 'mash' and 'vamp' Omar's verses, determined to produce good, readable poetry of his own, at any cost to accuracy and faithfulness. 'Better a live Sparrow than a stuffed Eagle' was his sensible motto. This deliberate policy of free-ranging adaptation has resulted in something substantially different from the originals. He described his quatrains as being 'tessellated into a sort of Epicurean Eclogue in a Persian Garden'; when they were finished they owed their oriental setting and basic ideas to Omar Khayyam (and other Persian poets), but the poetry was FitzGerald's, along with the new overall pattern and altered tone which they had acquired. It was his skill which brought an unsung Persian poet to international celebrity and returned him to his own people with a new crown. A greater debt is owed by the Persian to the Englishman than vice versa.

What are the poetic merits of these verses?

The Unified Poem

First, the reshaping of them. Out of the amorphous mass of Omar's rhymed but arbitrary philosophical musings FitzGerald has created an organised, elegantly shaped poem with a consistent theme and an expanding meaning. There can be no doubting the integrity of this 400-line masterpiece. It has the same gently curving structure as its comparable predecessor, Thomas Gray's *Elegy Written in a Country Churchyard* (1751), though the two works move in opposite directions. Gray begins in the evening and ends with the sunrise; FitzGerald moves from early morning to late evening. Through this encompassing device alone, both works achieve the kind of solid unity that is not put at risk by thoughtful digressions. But, of the two, FitzGerald's is the more coherent arrangement, even though his work is nearly four times the length of Gray's.

At the beginning he sets out his main theme, that of intoxication (more of which below), and he returns to this consistently, never abandoning it for more than a handful of stanzas. For instance, six of the first eight stanzas (all except 1 and 4) deploy the underlying theme of drinking, then we have three stanzas (9. 10, 11) that go off on their own, first reminding us of the fragility of life and then inviting us into a condition of such happiness that it will be the envy of the richest monarch. Stanza 12 (the best known of them all) describes what this is:

> A Book of Verses underneath the Bough,
> A Jug of Wine, a Loaf of Bread – and Thou
>   Beside me singing in the Wilderness –
> O Wilderness were Paradise enow!

This is the magic formula, a succinct and beautiful statement of Epicurean philosophy. The Greek philosopher Epicurus (c.341–270 BC) advocated the steady cultivation of pleasure, partly by eliminating pain and the fear of death (and not brutish sensuality, as has sometimes been implied). All you need for human happiness is expressed in the twenty-eight words of FitzGerald's stanza: a shady corner in nature, food and drink, company (which seems to mean love and hints at sex, to judge by the many erotic illustrations that have appeared) and culture, here represented by music and poetry. (Note the lack of what is now universally regarded in Western society as necessary for happiness: indoor, urban life directed towards celebrity, money and power.) If this be hedonism, let there be more of it; anyone who gets all of those ducks in line will certainly be happier than a sated sultan in his palace. We cannot fail to notice that the drink is alcoholic – the theme of intoxication has returned to warm us.

Unlikely to be forgotten, the main theme now disappears for ten stanzas (13–22) in which we are confronted, variously, with the fragility of life (again), the need to enjoy our present state, the elusiveness of hope for a better way of things, the permanence of death, its universal applicability, the shimmering possibility of reincarnation, and the sad vision of a beautiful palace now deserted except for a silly cooing bird. This has been so beautifully told, with such a deft touch, that the bad news is not likely to leave you feeling depressed at this stage (for reasons to which we shall return), but it would do if the poet went on inexorably with the same ideas. Once again relief is needed, and it can come from only one source – the cups of wine served up in stanzas 23 and 24. And this is how the poem works: a short succession of contemplative stanzas is always followed by a return to the main idea – that wine is needed to save us from sadness.

The groups of stanzas leading us away from and back to the main theme tend to have their own collective spirit. For instance, in the next section, after a couple of quatrains reminding us sadly of departed friends and the imminence of our own descent into darkness, we enter a particular realm of speculation that ought to set the seal on our hopelessness, though once again it does not quite manage to do so. Six splendid stanzas (28–33) give us more bad news: it is no good turning to our thinkers and teachers for an explanation of the human condition or guidance through it, because the brightest and best of them know absolutely nothing. These lofty experts, academic and spiritual, are brought before us in a derisory parade of personified human wisdom: Saints and Sages, Prophets, Philosopher and Doctor, Doctor and Saint, all of whose ideas and fine speeches amount to nothing more substantial than water and wind. (I, who have tried to read Heidegger, can say with assurance that in doing so I came out 'by the same Door as in I went' (see 31).) The poet reminds us that only Old Khayyam has the one true secret (30), and he has already told us what it is. Naturally, we need a drink of wine to digest this disappointment; we are offered 'Another and another Cup' in stanza 34.

After that, dimness, blindness and darkness conspire with death and fate to paint the human picture even darker; this is allowed to last for only four stanzas before the provision of relief. Once more we are invited to drink, this time by the lip of the vessel that offers itself, and with a clear statement that each of us should consider this offering 'the Secret of my Life' (39). Then come three stanzas (40–42) reiterating the slender possibility of reincarnation (though perhaps in less than human form), but the Cup is to hand in stanzas 43–45, and wine figures strongly in the next three. Quatrain 46 is a most beautiful statement of the best thing to do: accept the wine and with it enjoy the caresses of the lissom girl (or epicene boy, perhaps) who brings it:

> And lose your Fingers in the Tresses of
> The Cypress-slender Minister of Wine.

We are now virtually halfway through the poem, and the way ahead is clear. There is no need for further detailed commentary, though stanza 79 is worth lingering over, another one that contains the essence of the argument:

YESTERDAY *This* Day's Madness did prepare:
TOMORROW's Silence, Triumph, or Despair:
   Drink! for you know not whence you came, nor why:
Drink! for you know not why you go, nor where.

You may wonder why these last two lines are so stunningly effective. It is because of their exclamatory openings, the repetition of an entire half-line (anaphora), the staccato thrust of twenty successive monosyllables, and the gentle reversal of word order (chiasmus) which gives us 'whence . . . why' followed by 'why . . . where'. In these two lines alone we can see why A. S. Byatt tells us that 'FitzGerald's verse is insidiously memorable. It sings in the mind . . .' By the way, this stanza did not appear in the otherwise preferable first edition, so it could easily be missed by some readers (see Note on the Text).

One other passage deserves special mention because it stands out boldly from the main text by being given a named section of eight stanzas all to itself: *Kuza-Nama*, the Book of Pots.

It is distinctive and yet well integrated. Having been anticipated by several previous references to clay, potters and pots (41, 42, 49, 78), it also brings us to the end of our day-long excursion by recounting an evening event, with the moon about to appear, which prepares us for the crepuscular ending of the poem less than a dozen quatrains down the line. The narrator finds himself in a potter's shop, listening to the vessels as they speak to each other. They are discussing the ways of the ultimate Potter-Creator. In all the eight stanzas there is no denial of God, no querying of His existence, but that does not mean that His creation is happy and contented with what He has done. All the speaking pots (not all of them can speak) share a common degree of dissatisfaction with this potter who has formed them out of love but still got so many things wrong. Why has he allowed into his creation so much unfairness, imperfection and mystery? Why does he (like the Old Testament deity) behave so angrily, like a 'peevish Boy' (90)? No one calls the meeting to order, of course, and the poet does not summarise the argument. We have to do that for ourselves, and it seems to go like this. Creation is so obviously a rich, good and enjoyable thing that we must surely celebrate it, and pay tribute to the force that lies behind it. We shall have to live with the lack of clarity, the lack of perfection, the many injustices, but this is no reason to reject either life itself or the great Creative Power. Despite everything, God turns out to be a 'Good Fellow'. A similarly indulgent attitude to a deity that hides more than he shows has been displayed before, incidentally, in stanza 75, which makes this comment on the game of life:

> And He that tossed Thee down into the Field,
> *He* knows about it all – HE knows – **HE** knows!

On this occasion, naturally enough, we are brought back to the real world in the usual way. One of the pots has dried out, and calls out for lubrication in a nicely ambiguous phrase or two:

> But, fill me with the old familiar Juice,
> Methinks I might recover by-and-bye! (93)

He appears to crave liquid for the restoration of his desiccated clay tissues, but we all know what Bertie

Wooster means when he says to Jeeves, 'Fill me with the old familiar juice.'

In formal terms this unusual section works just like all the others. The quatrains wander away and find their way back, and, although the needs and reasons differ on each occasion, the resulting injunction is always the same: Drink!

Not much is left to tell. Quatrains 95–99 begin with Grape and end with Wine. The concluding section (100–105) is less optimistic than *Kuza-Nama*, but it is still a long way from despair. Annoyance (if only we could have a tiny glimpse of the truth . . .) is followed by a conclusion that the universe would need a lot of reshaping before we could ever find lasting happiness in it, and then we are at the end of the day, the end of life. In this poem the ending is exquisite. As in Gray's *Elegy* the death of the poet-narrator is signalled by his absence, which dawns upon an external observer. But whereas Gray entrusts this task to 'some hoary-headed swain', FitzGerald gives it to the Moon. The Moon looks down on humanity in a poignant image of someone looking for a lost individual. This is an astonishing ending: in spite of all that has gone, can it be that the absence of one individual might be noticed by an elemental force? There is an outdoor party; guests are 'Star-scattered' on the grass. (Where did he find that unforgettable adjective?) And the death of the poet is to be celebrated in the only way possible – by draining a glass of something strong. So the poem completes itself in the way that all of its subsections have done, by a return to our beginning. The cup that was being filled in the second quatrain is emptied again in the last one. Who would wish to dissent from the view of one critic, who says, 'The last two stanzas of the *Rubaiyat* shine with a lyrical beauty seldom matched in English literature'?

Let there be no mistake: this collection of quatrains is a poem in itself. The shapely wholeness of the *Rubaiyat* has been acknowledged by most writers and critics, including some as distinguished as T. S. Eliot and Ezra Pound, and since there is nothing like it in the Omarian original, this counts as one of the work's first claims to distinctiveness. Before looking closely at the next one – EFG's skill as a poet – we need to say a final word about the unifying theme of the poem.

Wine! Wine! Wine!

As we have seen, there is a lot of alcohol in the *Rubaiyat of Omar Khayyam*. It is the main preoccupation of the poem, the rallying-point around which everything unites. About a quarter of all the quatrains contain some reference to drinking. There are close on fifty specific references to the Cup, Glass, Drink, Jug, Wine, Tavern, Tapster, Vintner, Liquor, Draught, Juice, Vine, Grape, or Ruby vintage. Put like that, it begins to sound like an alcoholics' charter, but there is something wrong with this idea. Nowhere is there a call for the reader to run away from life, descend into an alcoholic stupor and stay there until called by the dark angel. Whatever is meant by alcohol, it must be something positive. The call is to drink and enjoy doing so, regularly, much of the time, morning and evening, but not to excess, not to invoke oblivion. If you did that, what would happen to the delicate balance recommended as the secret of happiness in quatrain 12? To get hopelessly drunk would be to neglect everything else that makes one happier than a sultan: the world of nature, bread, poetry and music, companionship and love. Neither Omar Khayyam nor Edward FitzGerald wants that to happen.

Almost none of the drinking is solitary. As at that final party (and the similar one, indoors, described in 24–25), imbibing usually seems to involve communion with others, and, in at least once case (46), enjoying the caresses of the one who delivers the wine, which would hardly be possible in a drunken state. Perhaps stanza 59 gives the advice that matters: '. . . be merry with the fruitful grape'. The positive effects of wine are laid out in stanzas 64 and 65: it has its own logic that can confute all arguments, it can change a life of lead into one of gold, it can scatter and slay all fears and sorrows. It is seen as more of a blessing than a curse (67), a means of recovery from depression (93), the vintner's 'precious goods', a necessary provision when people come together.

All of this contains an element of undeniable escapism. Drinking will enable us to forget yesterday and tomorrow, and to set aside the worries of the world. We should welcome a slight blurring of reality, to soften its edges, but not enough to send us to sleep, which would be a waste of time that could otherwise be enjoyed.

So, this is one way of understanding the meaning of wine in this poem; it is direct and obvious, and not too many people will want to take it much farther. After all, it amounts to the very 'material epicureanism' that Edward FitzGerald set out to express. But some have objected to this in the past, and others are likely to do so again. The commonest alternative reading is to see wine as a symbol of intoxication induced by divine love and spiritual joy. Some readers of the original quatrains (whether or not they can be definitively ascribed to Omar) are convinced that Persian poetry usually has a double meaning, and that Omar was the first great Sufi writer to build 'an inner castle of wisdom' within his quatrains. The first Westerner to take this line of thinking was a Frenchman, J. B. Nicolas, in 1867. FitzGerald himself rejected it out of hand, pointing out that plenty of people considered Omar Khayyam to be 'a great *opponent* of Sufism'; he also claims that although some quatrains seem to be unaccountable unless given a mystical interpretation, there are many more that obviously have nothing more than a literal meaning. Nevertheless, the Sufic approach has survived. In the 1930s an Indian monk, Paramahansa Yogananda, began publishing a series of Sufic interpretations of the *Rubaiyat*, which were gathered together into a book that was republished as recently as 1996. In the late 1960s a new translation by Robert Graves claimed to be 'a corrective presentation of the true Khayyam', whose work was full of hidden Sufic meanings. While writing his introduction Graves lost no opportunity to disparage FitzGerald as an inaccurate translator and incompetent versifier, though he ended up with egg on his face when his claim to have used a newly discovered manuscript of Omar Khayyam and written the definitive translation was completely discredited. So were his ill-judged criticisms of EFG, as time has continued to prove.

Not many readers will want to delve too deeply into

this controversy. The Sufic theory cannot be disproved, but we must surely take account of the English poet's intentions and achievement. He did not read Omar as a Sufic oracle, and his poem does not obviously convey this as a meaning. If any readers still wish to read Sufic allegory into the most popular long poem in our language, they are most welcome to do so, even if its author did not intend that. Graves pays EFG an unintended compliment when he accuses him of having 'constructed a mid-Victorian poem of his own'. This is exactly what we want to hear. These quatrains do indeed amount to a complete and distinctive poem, and they are more FitzGerald than Omar.

Making Game

One thing many people accept is that Edward FitzGerald contributed to the flow of pessimism that seeped into English life and culture in the nineteenth century and still seems to be with us. Did his most famous work not coincide exactly with Darwin's *Origin of Species* (1859), and nearly as closely with Tennyson's *In Memoriam* (1850), to produce a trio of mid-century works which undermined religious certainty while expressing the darkening mood of their generation, thus prefiguring the sombre thoughts of people like Arnold and Hardy? Did it not confirm the deep uncertainties of an age in which Schopenhauer and then Nietzsche called for 'strong pessimism'? Did FitzGerald not dismiss the human condition as a 'sorry Scheme of Things', telling us repeatedly that 'Worldly Hope . . . Turns Ashes', that our life is 'One Moment in Annihilation's Waste', and so on?

In fact, the *Rubaiyat of Omar Khayyam* is a poem that would barely register on any scale of pessimism known to mankind. Easy and pleasant to read and remember, it lifts the heart, and leaves you smiling. So, how does it happen that a hundred reminders of imperfection, impending death and permanent extinction prove for every last reader to be so diverting, inspiring and worth savouring in the memory year after year? This has to do with FitzGerald's personal delight in living, his attitude of incorrigible amusement and, most of all, the disarming power of his poetic style.

His infusion of humour into the melancholy musings of Omar Khayyam is his second masterstroke, and it was deliberate. He did this as a matter of habit, instinctively exploiting a tendency that was always there in his conversation, his letters and his more formal writings. Once, when writing about a French critic whom he quite admired, he added a significant aside: 'I think he wants *Humour* a little – which after all I believe we dull English have above all other people (unless Irish?)'. There is not a little pride in this; it gives him pleasure to belong to two tribal groupings who inherit humour with their lifeblood. This quality in the *Rubaiyat* has certainly been noticed – one American says, 'It is gaiety as well as gusto that makes the *Rubaiyat* the perfect companion' – but it has still to be fully acknowledged. FitzGerald's sense of humour completely determines the tone of this work, making philosophy fun, and turning the condition of the universe into a good joke that we can all share. These are the key lines:

But leave the Wise to wrangle, and with me
The Quarrel of the Universe let be:
   And, in some corner of the Hubbub coucht,
Make Game of that which makes as much of Thee. (66).

(The italics are ours, but they could well have been his because one of EFG's recurrent pleasantries was to play around with the typography of his poem, another original and amusing use of his material.)

This stanza has a curious background. First, it is one of the few for which no parallel has been discovered in Persian poetry; second, it was dropped after the first edition, and never reinstated by EFG. Why should that be? Most of the changes wrought by the poet on the almost unimprovable first edition were unfortunate ones. There is universal agreement with Swinburne that the first edition 'is the only one worth having'. It may be that the stanza was dropped out of misguided fidelity to Omar. This is a pity, because the quality of EFG's work increases in proportion as he departs from his original, and here we have another quatrain that contains part of essential argument. God and the Universe seem to treat us like a kind of cosmic joke; what better than to treat them the same way?

Making game is the true spirit of the *Rubaiyat*. The poem even includes a short section (73–75) on various amusements, mentioning the figures in a magic-lantern show, life seen as a game of chess and a sport that seems likely to be polo. This is a crystallisation of the general tone of amusement that characterises the *Rubaiyat* under FitzGerald's treatment. Further emphasis of this point can be provided by comparison with other writers.

Quatrain 66, because of its quirky humour, could never have appeared in comparable works such as Gray's *Elegy* or Housman's *A Shropshire Lad*. Conversely, here is a Housman quatrain that would be out of place in the *Rubaiyat*:

> They say my verse is sad: no wonder;
>   Its narrow measure spans
> Tears of eternity and sorrow,
>   Not mine, but man's.

This is Schopenhauer set to music, it cannot accommodate humour, and it could never have had a place in FitzGerald's world.

EFG's humour is, in the best sense, avuncular. The *Rubaiyat*, in FitzGerald's version, is the story of the apocalypse told to us by a kind uncle. Uncles sometimes tell poor jokes, but they are loved. Good and bad jokes decorate every page of this poem. Consider the feeble pun offered up in stanza 35: the poet has unravelled many knots, 'But *not* the *knot* of Human Death and Fate'.

Here is a bit of nonsense concerning a dove:

And 'Coo, coo, coo,' she cried; and 'Coo, coo, coo.' (22)

This may be compared with Robert Graves' (presumably) more accurate rendering of the original, which occupies the last stanza in his series of 111. He tells us of a tall palace, and the concluding words of his poem, devoid of all humour, significance and character, are:

A ring-dove perches on its battlements:

'Where, where?' it coos, 'where, where?'

Here, by contrast, is a whole FitzGerald stanza that, despite playing with a serious idea, is jokey in presentation:

For 'IS' and 'IS-NOT' though with Rule and Line,
And 'UP-AND-DOWN' by Logic I define,
    Of all that I should care to fathom, I
Was never deep in anything but – Wine. (61)

Some passages are so colloquial that they sound amusing whatever they are trying to say. For instance:

Ah, take the Cash in hand and waive the Rest;
O he brave Music of a *distant* Drum! (13)

and

Indeed the Idols I have loved so long
Have done my Credit in Men's Eye much wrong:
    Have drown'd my Honour in a shallow Cup
And sold my Reputation for a Song. (97)

and

Indeed, indeed, Repentance oft before
I swore – but was I sober when I swore? (98)

This language is so chatty one can hardly believe that serious ideas are in play, though they usually are. The

moment a serious thought begins to assert itself, FitzGerald will begin his next stanza in the most casual way:
'But come with old Khayyam . . .'; When you and I . . .';
'I think . . .'; 'You know, my friends . . .'; 'I tell thee this
. . .'; 'And this I know . . .'; 'And look . . .'; 'I sometimes
think . . .'; 'I often wonder . . .' These expressions are not
fillers packing out the lines with the right number of
syllables. They are deliberate devices used to hold the
poem down; poetry and philosophy can be high flown
and difficult, and EFG does not want that to happen here.
His conversational tone, gently amusing, gives an
impression of lightness, continually reassuring the reader
that everything in this work is pleasurable, there will be
nothing formidable either from the ideas or the poetry.

On a higher level of sophistication but still on the edge
of jokiness, the letter 'w' achieves its apotheosis in
stanzas 32–34. Look at these words: 'With . . . Wisdom
. . . sow . . . with . . . own . . . grow . . . was . . . Water . . .
Wind . . . why . . . knowing . . . whence . . . Water willy-
nilly flowing . . . Wind . . . Waste . . . whither, willy-nilly
blowing . . . What, without . . . whence . . . without . . .
whither . . .' – all that (24 x 'w') in ten lines, deliberately
overdone, deliberately amusing, and despite dealing with
a profound philosophical problem.

'The Wine of Life keeps oozing drop by drop . . .' is an
obvious and amusing reference to Keats's ode 'To
Autumn'. Shakespeare is cheerily invoked by the line
'Sans Wine, sans Song, sans Singer, and – sans End!',
and this example could scarcely be more appropriate.
Jaques's famous speech in *As You Like It*, beginning 'All
the world's a stage . . .' and ending with 'Sans teeth, sans
eyes, sans taste, sans everything', is a perfect example of

what we are discussing. Everybody feels a frisson of excitement as this famous speech begins, and audiences go home with the lovely poetry ringing in their ears – the schoolboy with his 'shining morning face', and so on. They may not have noticed, or they do not care to dwell on, the actual content of the speech, which is a thoroughly dispiriting account of human life in all its seven stages. Fine language distracts, uplifts and reduces despair to melancholy. By this means EFG is able to present the business of life not as a painful tragedy inherent in the death sentence that is each person's birthright, but a glorious thrill and a good joke. Our sadness derives not from the awfulness of living, but from too much enjoyment of it. Much of this thinking derives from the Persian, of course, but there can be little doubt that the flavour of the English version depends upon the poetic authority of FitzGerald's lovely pentameters. The quatrains may be read and recalled by any person in any mood, always with a positive outcome.

The Poetry of FitzGerald's *Rubaiyat*

A little more needs to be said about FitzGerald's poetry. His memorable stanza is nothing less than sensational: a quatrain rhyming *aaba*, a glorious innovation in English letters. True, it was borrowed from Omar, who seems to have adopted it sometimes in order to defy a tedious Persian tradition of quatrains in which all four lines shared the same rhyme. The origin is thus Persian, but FitzGerald has adapted it to his own needs. Omar's quatrains are exactly that: four lines which build a little argument steadily line by line to a striking culmination. FitzGerald's have a different character. Pulling against the four-line structure so obvious on the page is a *three-part* argument created by continual binding of the first two lines into a strong couplet. The *aa* rhyme encourages this and nothing is done to resist it; on the contrary, most stanzas end line 2 with strong punctuation, and a sense of completion. More often than not you simply have to take the opening couplet as a single proposition. For instance: ''Tis all a Chequer-board of Nights and Days / Where Destiny with Men for Pieces plays' (74); 'O Thou, who didst with Pitfall and with Gin / Beset the Road I was to wander in' (85); 'That ev'n my buried Ashes such a Snare / Of Perfume shall fling up into the Air' (96).

As in the last example, enjambement sometimes stitches the two lines tightly together.

Frequently, a first-line subject finds its verb in the second-line, or a verb its object: 'Morning . . . / Has flung . . .' (1); 'Those who stood . . . / . . . shouted . . .' (3); 'Myself . . . did . . . frequent / Doctor and Saint . . .' (31), and so on.

The wholeness of the opening couplet helps to offset the third line, which is already pleasantly dislocated by being indented at the beginning and differently rhymed. The looping away of this impertinent line, only for it to be recaptured by the last line and locked up by the final rhyme – this is the great charm of the quatrain. But it is not the change of rhyme at line 3 that creats the real shock – at first sight this looks like the beginning of another couplet – so much as the surprise created when the third rhyme pops up again at the end of line 4, uniquely in English poetry. It comes as a wonderful frisson in almost every stanza that the last word does not rhyme with the line before but the one before that, and the one before that. Even when you know it is coming, it still surprises. This form is a welcome injection of freshness into the most familiar form used by English poetry. The good old quatrain, which even appears as a building block in most sonnets, is the most popular of all stanzaic forms, so natural to us that it has been described as projecting a deep and permanent appeal to human nature. It is astonishing that anyone could have rejuvenated this ancient instrument with such effectiveness as late as the mid-nineteenth century.

The celebrated opening stanza illustrates to a nicety all of the characteristics described above (some of which do not derive from the Persian):

> Awake! for Morning in the Bowl of Night
> Has flung the Stone that puts the Stars to Flight:
>   And Lo! the Hunter of the East has caught
> The Sultan's Turret in a Noose of Light. (1)

This unique, captivating formula repeats itself with infinitely renewable freshness, mildly spiced by occasional slight departures from the basic pattern. It is enhanced by FitzGerald's special language – a delicious blending of archaisms, self-conscious poeticisms, exclamations, asides, superb and exotic metaphors, direct speech, apostrophe, real and rhetorical questions, striking examples of chiasmus, repetitions, listings, emphases, colloquial interjections, and even typographical innovations. This bravura display is a significantly richer mixture of poetical imagery and rhetoric than belongs to the Persian originals. Omar's stanzas appear to be lean and spare; another translator, Peter Avery (with much better knowledge of the language), tells us that it seemed to him important 'to try and convey the baldness of the originals'. FitzGerald himself knows what he has left behind: 'Omar's Simplicity, which is so much a Virtue in him'. This virtual apology, in a letter to Cowell, for something that was done deliberately and amounted to a substantial improvement, is a sadly amusing indication of the English poet's reticence. Without his generous stylistic embellishment no one would have heard of Omar Khayyam's unadorned verses.

The gentle dexterity of FitzGerald's rhyming is another source of delight. To combine three similar rhymes over and over again while making them seem natural and fresh is a difficult matter in English, which is not conducive to easy multiple rhyming. FitzGerald's triple rhymes are so good that no one notices them, the trick being to avoid rhyming the same part of speech whenever possible. Not a few stanzas manage three different parts of speech: sky, cry, dry (2); bough, thou, enow (12); writ, wit, it (76), and, by the way, several stanzas use *four* similar rhymes, *aaaa* (e.g. 11, 30, 36, 74), but it is a safe bet that nobody ever notices them. No critic seems to have singled them out for comment. It is the sensitive and original use of all these resources which gives FitzGerald's pentameters a supple dynamism and sharp individuality sufficient to mark him out as an outstanding poet.

The Patron Saint of Merrymaking?

None of this makes it easy to find a proper place for Edward FitzGerald in the family of our literature. One thing is sure: he has been undervalued. He can be compared directly to Thomas Gray and A. E. Housman, who have not. All three were quiet, reclusive, modest, conservative, homosexuals (living at a time when you couldn't even think of such things), classical scholars, who produced a small volume of quatrains that took off and went round the world, but wrote little beyond that. Of the three it was EFG who sold the most and became the best known, but this has not helped him posthumously. Gray and Housman have been showered with honours: they have their statues, memorials (in Westminster Abbey and elsewhere), appreciation societies and websites. EFG lies neglected in an unkempt Suffolk graveyard that is difficult even to find. For him 'www' means water, wind and wisdom. He was omitted from a recent history of English poetry that ran to a thousand pages and described the work of a thousand poets. How can we put this right?

The first obstacle to be disposed of is the contention, usually implicit, that a mere translation cannot count as a proper English poem. FitzGerald was not a mere translator. His attitude to this kind of work was explained on numerous occasions, but its clearest expression came in that same letter to Cowell (27 April 1859), in which he wrote, 'I suppose very few People have ever taken such Pains in Translation as I have, but certainly not to be literal.' This should be set against Vladimir Nabokov's claim about literal translation: 'Only this is true translation.' FitzGerald is about as untrue as you can get without departing remotely from the original. When Nabokov admits he sacrificed 'everything (elegance, euphony, clarity, good taste, modern usage, and even grammar)' to his ideal of literalism, he is measuring the great strides taken by EFG in the opposite direction. FitzGerald is determined to sacrifice literalism for all the things Nabokov dispensed with, and more. The *Rubaiyat of Omar Khayyam* should now be accepted, once and for all, both as a complete entity and a valid literary achievement which, although derivative, has enough originality and technical skill to bear comparison with the best work of many other English poets whose significance is never doubted. Not to do that would be illogical. Matthew Arnold's poem 'Sohrab and Rustum' (1852) is criticised on a number of counts, but nobody assesses its value in terms of faithfulness to the Persian poet Firdausi, from whom it derives. When people point to the King James Bible as some of the finest English ever written, they are not thinking in terms of its fidelity as a translation. And what about Chaucer and Shakespeare – although they are not translators, shouldn't we castigate them for excessive reliance on earlier writers, many of them *foreign*, for ideas, plots, situations and characters? We do not do so because they transcended their original material, which is what FitzGerald, in a different way and on a smaller scale, has also done.

It has been claimed that FitzGerald liberated Omar Khayyam from oriental obscurity only to trap the Persian in a role as the patron saint of merrymaking. Is this the level on which we should place EFG himself? This would hardly be enough. We have tried to present the *Rubaiyat* as an unusually accomplished, clever, unified and attractive work of English poetry, one of the most memorable ever written. Originality and skill these stanzas have in abundance, when considered as poetry. Their ideas, on the other hand, are neither original nor profound. It is not exactly new to remind readers of the shortness and fragility of human life, and tell them to enjoy themselves before it is too late. Compared with Tennyson's *In Memoriam*, a desperate and painful struggle with personal loss and eroding religious faith, the *Rubaiyat* seem to have little to offer beyond amusement. The poet has deliberately played down the seriousness of his endeavour. Even so, for all the insouciance of their presentation, there certainly are serious ideas in the *Rubaiyat*, not enough perhaps to change people's lives, but enough to make them think a little about the one they are leading, and to enjoy it more.

Edward FitzGerald may not be in the same league as Tennyson or Shakespeare or the other major English-language poets, but no one has ever claimed that he is. When a critic describes EFG's work as 'so felicitous, so Schubert-like in the excellence of its poetry', he is not comparing him with Mozart or Beethoven. Conversely, it cannot be right to dismiss this writer as inconsequential when set alongside the much larger galaxy of highly regarded poets of the second rank. There is no need to name names beyond those already mentioned, but Edward FitzGerald should be willingly accepted into the upper echelons of their group, and confirmed as one who deserved his enormous popularity, which has been achieved without descending to doggerel or sentimentality. He wrote with great skill and poetic discernment. As it happens, there is one other work written by him that confirms his ability.

Bird Parliament

Bird Parliament is a hidden treasure, a masterpiece that is virtually unknown. It appears in no books of quotations, no general anthologies, no learned studies. Hardly anyone has even heard of it. The reason for its neglect lies, once again, in the diffidence of its author. FitzGerald may have insisted on issuing the *Rubaiyat* anonymously, but *Bird Parliament* suffered worse: it was never offered for publication. After his death it emerged in print only as part of a three-volume miscellany with the unalluring title *Letters and Literary Remains* (1889). Unnoticed at the time, it has since then never been brought to prominence, let alone published singly or alongside the *Rubaiyat of Omar Khayyam*. Reissued in 1962, again in a large miscellany, it attracted no attention, just as no one had celebrated its presentation, severely truncated, in a collection of Persian poetry in 1954.

Yet the quality of this work is remarkable, and clearly evident at the first reading. It is a narrative poem with a double storyline; as the underlying narrative gathers force, a series of short, interpolated tales entertain us in passing. *Bird Parliament* is another 'translation' from the Persian. *Mantik ut-Tair* (*Speeches of the Birds*) was written by a successor of Omar Khayyam, Farrid ud-Din Attar. A prolific writer, of the Sufic persuasion within Islam, Attar counted the *Mantik* as one of his most successful works; it is widely accepted as an ingenious illustration of Paradise attained by the absorption of the Sufi into the Deity itself. If this sounds rather portentous, we can be reassured by FitzGerald's attitude to the poem. He determined not to translate all of the vast original, but to give a 'Bird's-Eye view of the Bird Poem', which in any case already enjoyed 'the advantage of having a Story to hang all upon'. The *story* of this poem was seen as its first quality, and heaviness of style was to be avoided at all costs. FitzGerald reduced the original 4500 lines to a more digestible 1435, redirecting its energy and giving a new tone. Comparing his work with the full text (translated in 1984 as *The Conference of the Birds*), who could fail to admire the boldness with which he has cut his own swathe through the wordiness and repetitious austerity of the original?

The birds come together in a great congregation to elect a leader. A spiritually advanced lapwing, the Tajidar, takes command as their self-appointed overlord and talks of a great quest which they must undertake in order to achieve bliss in the afterlife. Most of the birds are not up to the challenge, but a few of them do set out, and in the end only thirty arrive at the destination, after terrible ordeals and discouragements. They are eventually absorbed into the One True Essence.

This spiritual journey may be the ultimate purpose of the poem, but it is far from being the whole story. Of more immediate interest is the series of engaging self-portraits created as the birds step forward to present themselves. Their descriptions, antics and attitudes are so amusing that they could easily be presented to small children, though they also happen to deliver such a broad range of recognisably human weaknesses that their narrative rises to the heights of smiling satirical portraiture. Although continuously aware of a great avian company in the background, we are entertained directly by a dozen particular birds who speak for themselves, presenting varied personalities in an unforgettably charming sequence.

All the birds assert their own virtues and the superiority of their particular way of life. Most want to stay where they are, because they are doing very nicely, thank you. The one or two who approve of the journey do so for the wrong reasons. They want to gain more treats or to have some minor deficiency put right so that life will be better still: for example, the Peacock knows himself for a thing of rare beauty but he does admit to having ugly feet. All of this is humorously *wrong*; the Tajidar keeps reminding them that the only way to Fulfilment involves giving up worldly pleasures, not increasing them. Much delight accrues for the reader from their mundane ordinariness, which keeps bumping up against his stern spirituality. More still flows from the disparities between the individual birds and the certainty of each one of them that he is the only bird living a proper life. The instinctive conservatism of their species, and ours, has rarely been more effectively satirised.

Portraits and Poetry

This aviary deserves to acquire lasting fame; its citizens ought to become famous as a set of amusing archetypes.

The admirable Pheasant is the only bird brave enough to question the authority of the new leader; he does so with exemplary courage and clear-sightedness. The besotted Nightingale, who is capable of nothing beyond ecstatic absorption in his Rose, contrasts with the sensuous Parrot, green, gold and greedy. The narrow-minded Owl, with his nocturnal miserliness, stands opposed to the smug Partridge, who digs for and eats rubies, which give him an enviable bodily glow. The Shah-Falcon and the Phoenix absurdly draw hand-me-down pleasure from association with royalty. Could anyone be more self-satisfied than these last three birds? As it happens, the Duck could. Does he not perform more fastidious ablutions than anyone else? Surely his washing routine guarantees his purity: 'Methinks I am the Saint of all our Tribe' (line 466). All of them outshine the puny Sparrow, so modestly attired in body and mind, and also the pathetic Ringdove, incapable of anything more than a plaintive call to a lost friend. (See stanza 22 of the *Rubaiyat of Omar Khayyam*, where he puts in a delightful guest appearance.) This varied company is made up, not of villains or rogues, but of ordinary creatures who are trying to do the best they can with what they have. Add together their shortcomings and you arrive at a sorry statement of the avian-human condition. We are made of silliness, fear and imperfection.

Monsters we are not, but our names are written in overweening pride, small-town smugness, sensuality, materialism, miserly concentration, obsequiousness, unwarranted self-esteem, self-pity, self-abasement and a shallow concern for external surface and display. It is fortunate that, although the Tajidar and the Lord of

Heaven are stern and solemn judges in these matters, our narrator is not. His geniality saves the day, rendering these characters acceptable and even lovable. For all their failings, they are a pleasant company: it is not difficult to sympathise with their simple aspirations, worries and fears. They are mostly ours too.

As in the *Rubaiyat*, FitzGerald's benevolent nature determines the tone of the whole poem. His humour often flashes forth in bursts of fine poetry. Take, for instance, this splendid entry:

Then came the subtle *Parrot* in a coat
Greener than Greensward, and about his Throat
A Collar ran of sub-sulphureous Gold;
And in his Beak a Sugar-Plum he troll'd,
That all his Words with luscious Lisping ran . . . (250–254)

An alternative, much more accurate, translation reads: 'The pretty parrot was the next to speak, / Clothed all in green with sugar in her beak . . .' This shows the extent of EFG's transformation. His lines seem almost too succulent for their own good, yet the exuberant language suits both the Parrot's high colouring and his cocky awareness of displaying such rare splendour. (FitzGerald kept a parrot, Beauty Bob, and knew whereof he wrote.) He can even risk an outrageous epithet like 'sub-sulphureous', which scarcely exists as a word; 'sulphureous' itself would have been remarkable. Rarer still, however, is the invention used to describe a miser who returns to earth in mouse-like form to scratch among the walls of his own house: 'But wherefore, Sir, so metamousified?' When a party of Moths, having done their work, return home, they report to the 'Chief of Mothistan'. When the fastidious Duck is called up, we read that 'from a pond / Waddled the dapper Duck, demure, adept . . .' Slapping feet can be heard in the dib-dab-dib of the consonants, six *d*s in as many words. And if you want an example of sheer amusing nonsense, try to imagine a two-syllable word chopped into halves by an intervening couplet. Here is the pathetic Ringdove, calling for Yusuf (Joseph):

> Then from a Wood was heard unseen to coo
> The Ringdove – 'Yusuf! Yusuf! Yusuf! Yu—'
> (For thus her sorrow broke her Note in twain,
> And, just where broken, took it up again)
> '—suf! Yusuf! Yusuf! Yusuf!' . . . (505–509)

Tricks and jokes like these may not be the hallmark of a great poet, but they do suggest a clever craftsman, and one who intends to entertain as much as to edify. But this poem also contains outbursts from that same genius which is recognised in the Omar Khayyam adaptations. At his best FitzGerald can sound almost Shakespearean, as when the Nightingale says

> I hang the Stars with Meshes for Men's Souls:
> The Garden underneath my Music rolls. (206–207)

or when we are told of the Supreme Shah in Heaven

> Who from his Throne above for certain Ends
> Awhile some Spangle of his Glory lends
> To Men on Earth . . . (448–450)

or in the depiction of human life as frighteningly precarious:

> For like a Child sent with a fluttering Light
> To feel his way along a gusty Night
> Man walks the World ... (685–687)

A more sustained display of poetic quality may be identified in lines 894–907, beginning 'And as the World upon her victims feeds ...', a wonderfully awful extended spider metaphor illustrating the vanity of human existence, sonnet-like, though written in couplets and with sufficient enjambement to blur the metrics beyond the grasp of memory. The same theme is taken up again on the following page, this time using a metaphor from the fisherman's trade:

> And if so vain the glittering Fish we get,
> How doubly vain to dote upon the Net,
> Call'd Life, that draws them, patching up this thin
> Tissue of Breathing out and Breathing in ... (952–955)

Nothing in the *Rubaiyat of Omar Khayyam* surpasses the sharp, sad beauty of these images that speak so poignantly of our small, transient, misspent lives.

The Stories

Then there are interpolated stories, more numerous than the characters, which emanate from a benign outsider who steps in frequently with a little adventure or parable to illustrate and reinforce a piece of advice. These miniature narratives (in this version, unlike the original, none is longer than a page or so, four of them are close to sonnet-size, and several are smaller than that) vary in length, content, gravity and relevance, but especially in the balance struck between entertainment and instruction. Several are overtly instructional, like the first one (94–108), which tells how Bajazyd fell under the spell of the night sky and wondered at the great mystery of it all. A Voice from Heaven warns him that the mystery is explained to very few. God says,

And ev'n of those who at my Portal din,
Thousands may knock for one that enters in. (107–108)

This is all precept and no story; it sets a dour tone. Most of the interpolated tales are not like that. Even when they instruct, they delight by entertainment; it is usually difficult to predict the outcome. The tone varies from tale to tale. Here is a happy story in which the Shah helps a young fisherman who is having no luck at his trade; he is rewarded by proper gratitude. There we read how the Shah, strolling incognito round his city, visits the baths and befriends a furnaceman, who passes every test of charity and good living. Elsewhere, God punishes Yusuf's father in a draconian manner simply because he will not stop continually moaning about his loss. Then we are told of the most heartless discouragement, in which a famous beauty, slavishly adored by an admirer who once encountered her smile, puts him down in cruel fashion:

Again she smiled and said, 'O self-beguiled
Poor Wretch, *at* whom and not *on* whom I smiled.' (248–249)

There is no shortage of ghastly occurrences. The Shah salutes prison staff who throw dismembered corpses before him over the prison wall; their diligent work of execution demonstrates that they are carrying out his orders assiduously. The Queen of Egypt wins the prize for brutal intolerance when, after challenging a passionate admirer to give up his life as the price of one night spent with her, she strikes him dead on the spot for even hesitating.

Such are the stories. You cannot imagine the larger narrative without them. They serve several purposes – to vary the shape and pace of the overall narrative, to entertain in their own right, and often to point up a moral truth which has until then received only general affirmation. Their rhythm and style are agreeable, alternating as they do with the endearing bird portraits. But they are not the main aim of *Bird Parliament*, which ultimately has a religious purpose.

At first sight the spiritual content of the poem may seem remote from our experience in the modern West. Some of its oriental symbolism is beyond our immediate understanding, and in any case the adventures of a few dozen questing birds do not seem liable to tell us much about ultimate reality. Nevertheless, there is food for thought here, even for the occidental mind.

The poem is full of intriguing ideas. Some are openly religious and therefore likely to be dismissed out of hand in our secular age; they should not be. The Tajidar tells us repeatedly that this life is not the only possibility that exists; it is a pale reflection of some greater entity of which we are also a part. We are shadows of some enormous force which even he in his wisdom is hard put to identify – it is the Creative Will, the Fount of Being, the Great Mystery. All sense and matter will return to the clay from which it was created, but new creation will flow from that event. Death is not to be dreaded. This life is a wearisome exile, from which we should seek deliverance, preparing for the great moment of self-annihilation when we shall look upon Infinity in a blaze of glory too powerful for us to confront except through a mirror.

The birds, like us, baulk at these lofty thoughts, and just want to get on with their lives. Their prevarication and excuses for not being quite ready for the great quest are a delight to read; we shall squirm to recognise our own nature in them:

> And much they long'd to go at once – but some,
> They said, so unexpectedly had come
> Leaving their Nests half-built – in bad Repair
> With Children in – Themselves about to pair –
> 'Might he not choose a better Season – nay,
> Better perhaps a Year or Two's Delay,
> Till all was settled, and themselves more stout
> And strong to carry their Repentance out –
> And then . . .' (799–807)

Passages like this show both the skill and the human-ity of the narrator. His ultimate interest may be in the next world, but his instincts and feelings are still close to ours in this one. Not so the Tajidar, who persists in his blandishments. Apart from his many little stories, he has three major speeches (lines 38–93, 562–625, 848–963). They may seem too long, but FitzGerald has already slashed Attar's poem by two-thirds, and we cannot ask him to do more. They should be persisted with, as should also the long journey of the birds, as a reflection of the arduous pilgrim's progress which has to be undertaken. In any case, they contain rich wisdom and splendid verses.

The journey of the birds extends over six pages and two hundred lines (1147–1358), including some dense passages worthy of reading more than once. Birds and humans blend together, wings ache and feet bleed. It is almost as difficult to describe the end of the quest as it is for the narrators to convey their idea of God or Heaven. In pragmatic terms the birds arrive at their destination and are admitted to paradise. Just before admission they gain a curious sense of changing essence. In a wonderful scene of transfiguration thirty birds become the thirty-bird *Symurgh* (see Notes, p. 79), which has been drawing them on all the time. Self blends into otherness: seer and seen are identical. Fading individuality glimpses Infinity through the mirror only to pass through it into the new Realty: 'The Sun of my Perfection is a Glass / Wherein from *Seeing* into *Being* pass' (1401–1402). The conscious rays which once went out have now returned to their source. Hence the closing words of the poem proper:

Come and lost Atoms to your Centre draw,
And *be* the Eternal Mirror that you saw:
Rays that have wander'd into Darkness wide
Return, and back into your Sun subside. (1426–1429)

This is more than mere mysticism, or exotic oriental mumbo-jumbo. For one thing, these thoughts are strikingly similar, beneath their poetic language, to present-day concepts of how the universe was formed and what its future may be. Cosmologists speak nowadays of our emergence from, and possible return to, a 'singularity'. Line 1216 of *Bird Parliament* puts this concept most succinctly: 'The Universe that to a Point congeals'.

The clearest lesson to be drawn from this remarkable poem is that, at the very least, there is something illusory and mysterious about the human condition which cannot be worked out in logical propositions. In lines 1248–1260 we are invited by the prophet to build a great pyre of all that keeps us from the greater reality. Everything must go on to it: 'Irrelevant Ambitions, Lusts and Prides, Glory and Gold and sensual Desire. . . . All old Relations and Regards of Kin. . . . Rags and Integuments of Creeds out-worn . . .' Before the immolation of the self there is one last item to be disposed of:

> And top the giddy Summit with the Scroll
> Of *Reason* that in dingy Smoke shall roll
> Over the true Self-sacrifice of Soul. (1258–1260)

When Omar Khayyam said that he had 'Divorced old barren Reason from [his] bed' (60), he did so for epicurean purposes. Attar now does the same, but for philosophical ones, asserting that human reason, which lacks any power to explain ultimate mysteries, must eventually be abandoned. This is inspiring advice for our age, obsessed as it is with reductionist certainties and the algorithmic processing of ideas.

What is *Bird Parliament?* A long narrative poem filled with the richest materials: captivating satirical portraiture, stories galore, much humour and memorable poetry, skilful versification (in the form of heroic couplets and pleasant variations), an admirable sense of construction, an epic theme and profoundly important ideas. This masterpiece has been too long hidden from the reading public, because of the author's excessive modesty. Worthy of a high place in the pantheon of English narrative verse, it presents further confirmation of FitzGerald's unique poetic genius.

TONY BRIGGS

Note on the Texts

The *Rubaiyat of Omar Khayyam*

Edward FitzGerald's adaptation of Omar Khayyam's *Rubaiyat* exists in five different original editions approved by the author. The first and last are often published together since neither is adquate alone. Here, we publish a conflation of these editions, for the following reasons.

FitzGerald completed his first versions at the end of 1857, and in January 1858 he submitted some of them to *Fraser's Magazine*, withholding several stanzas that he considered liable to offend public taste. The editor kept them for nearly a year without making a decision. They were first published, by Bernard Quaritch, in April 1859 in the form of a pamphlet containing only seventy-five stanzas. Some of the missing quatrains were restored at this time, and when later editions appeared still others were added, along with a large number of alterations introduced by the author-translator. By the time of his death there were four redactions; a fifth was derived, in 1889, from an annotated copy with yet more corrections, and this is accepted as FitzGerald's last pronouncement on the subject. When the work is republished in only one version it is often this fifth edition which appears, though sometimes editors go back to the beginning and publish the incomplete first edition singly.

If we know the author's final decisions, why bother to publish anything other than the fifth edition? The simplest answer is that, by common acknowledgement, the overall poetic quality of the very first edition was not improved by the corrections. (The poet Swinburne speaks for us all when claiming that the first edition is 'the only one worth having'; one reviewer accused the revising author of having 'grievously injured the Original'.) FitzGerald seems to have thought, for example, that his text might be enhanced by removing from his first version some of the archaisms and exclamations, but these are an essential contribution to the sense of exoticism that gives the first edition its piquant flavour. The famous opening stanza illustrates the point. Its first version contains two extravagant metaphors and an exclamatory 'And Lo! . . .'; without these, the opening stanza of the later editions seems disappointingly feeble. Other changes were equally misguided. The author himself knew this to be true, as he once admitted: 'I dare say Edn 1 is better in some respects than 2, but I think not altogether.' This is the truth of it. The first edition has the finest poetry, but it deserves to be lengthened by additions, and in places it can be improved by small amendments. Fidelity to the Persian original is not at issue here. Much to his credit, the translator decided at an early stage to take Omar Khayyam, with whom he sensed a warm fellow-feeling, and 'vamp him up again with a few Alterations and Additions'. 'As to the relative fidelity of the [first] two editions', he later wrote, 'there isn't a Pin to choose.' Similarly, the selection of stanzas makes no real impact on the arrangement of ideas presented by the *Rubaiyat*. There is no logical sequence of any kind in the original Persian, which treated the quatrains as individual entities to such an extent that they were grouped in alphabetical order. FitzGerald's arrangement offers more in the way of overall shape – this is one of his important changes. (See the Introduction.) He has selected a suitable early-morning opening stanza (which false legend has often claimed to be his invention) and also an appropriate terminal one. Within the collection there are one or two runs of quatrains that are clearly interconnected, notably the potter's section entitled *Kuza-Nama* (stanzas 87–94): there is even an example of two stanzas being so closely linked in meaning that the one runs into the other without any intervening punctuation (80/81). Nevertheless, the pattern of thoughts is not much affected by slight rearrangement.

Where does this leave us? If you read the first edition you get the best poetry, whereas the other editions all provide a fuller text. But the common practice of publishing two different editions together is hardly the perfect answer. This may satisfy the scholarly reader who is prepared to do some cross-checking, but many editions already exist for his or her close scrutiny. What seems likely is that most people will read part or all of one edition, probably the first (since it is there at the beginning of the book), and not bother to penetrate much farther. Such people will miss some splendid lines. Who wants the *Rubaiyat* without such ringing monosyllabic phrases as these?

Drink! for you know not whence you came, nor why:
Drink! for you know not why you go, nor where. (79)

Many such memorable lines exist only in the later

editions. The obvious solution to this problem is to publish the first edition *incorporating the stanzas that were added later*. Quality and quantity are thus guaranteed. Even this, however, falls short of the ideal. What of those few stanzas that were manifestly *improved* by FitzGerald's corrections? Here is an example. The rather ugly lines of edition one

> I yet in all I only cared to know
> Was never deep in anything but – Wine. (one, 41)

are replaced in edition five by

> Of all that one should care to fathom, I
> Was never deep in anything but – Wine. (five, 56)

The simplification of syntax, together with a newly created and welcome enjambement, 'I / Was ...', amounts to a clear improvement, and should thus be allowed in. Similarly, the lines

> You know, my Friends, how long since in my House
> For a new Marriage did I make Carouse (one, 40)

are improved by FitzGerald's amendment:

> You know, my Friends, with what a brave Carouse
> I made a Second Marriage in my house. (five, 55)

Such textual improvements ought not to be disallowed simply because of the overall poetic superiority of the first edition.

On these principles this edition has been founded. It contains 105 quatrains, most of them (sixty-nine) straight from the first edition, but with numerous additions and a few amendments taken from the fifth (most involving small stylistic improvements). No fundamental changes have been made: all the lines and all the quatrains were actually written by Edward FitzGerald. The possibility of hybridisation by adding the first half of one quatrain to the second half of its corresponding variant, although tempting in places, has been resisted. A dozen stanzas were included in the second edition but dropped from subsequent ones; in general we have honoured the omissions, though three of these stanzas have been reinstated, both because of their intrinsic quality (especially 29) and because they contain interesting cross-references to certain lines in *Bird Parliament* (17 and 22).

The provenance of each stanza is given in the Notes.

It is common practice for transliterations from Persian into English to include, for accuracy, accents and other diacritical signs. Their meaning will probably seem obscure to the general reader and they have accordingly been omitted from this edition.

Bird Parliament

FitzGerald first took up Attar's *Bird Parliament* in late 1856. He refers to it in a letter of 22 January 1857 to Edward Cowell; impressed by its overall narrative strength and its 'illustrative Stories', he plans to make a 'Poetic Abstract' of the work. Later correspondence describes his determination to cut the original down to about half its size, though in the event he went much farther than that, ending up with about a quarter. Unimpressed by the structure or the poetry of the original, he displays confidence in his own ability to 'make some things readable which others have left unreadable'.

By the end of 1857 his adaptation of the poem was completed, but he had already assured Cowell that he had no intention of boring the world with his modest effort. *Bird Parliament* was never offered for publication, but one of FitzGerald's letters contains what looks like an oblique plea for posterity to cast an eye on his offering. 'I have put away the Mantic,' he wrote. 'When I die, what a farrago of such things will be found! Enough of such matter . . .'. *Bird Parliament* was finally issued by Aldis Wright in *Letters and Literary Remains* in 1889. It was published in severely abbreviated form by Everyman in an *Anthology of Persian Verse Translation* (1954 and 1986). Its full version appeared in Joanna Richardson's *FitzGerald: Selected Works* (Rupert Hart-Davis, 1962). The entire text of Attar's poem was published in a translation by Afkham Darbandi and Dick Davis as *The Conference of the Birds* (Penguin, 1984). Davis, one of the very few critics who knows FitzGerald's version of this poem, confirms that he 'translates very freely indeed', but still captures 'much of the tone and feeling of the original'. Another complete translation, *The Speech of the Birds*, by Peter Avery, was published in 1998. Neither of these versions would have had much chance of achieving wide popularity, not only because the translators cannot match the poetic skill of Edward FitzGerald, but also because they have kept discouragingly to the full length of the original.

Omar Khayyam

The Rubaiyat of Omar Khayyam

1

Awake! for Morning in the Bowl of Night
Has flung the Stone that puts the Stars to Flight:*
    And Lo! the Hunter of the East has caught
The Sultan's Turret in a Noose of Light.

2

Dreaming when Dawn's Left Hand* was in the Sky
I heard a Voice within the Tavern cry,
    'Awake, my Little ones, and fill the Cup
'Before Life's Liquor in its Cup be dry.'

3

And as the Cock crew, those who stood before
The Tavern shouted – 'Open then the Door!
    'You know how little while we have to stay,
'And, once departed, may return no more.'

4

Now the New Year reviving old Desires,
The thoughtful Soul to Solitude retires,
    Where the WHITE HAND OF MOSES* on the Bough
Puts out, and Jesus from the Ground suspires.*

5

Iram* indeed is gone with all its Rose
And Jamshyd's Sev'n-ring'd Cup* where no one knows;
    But still the Vine her ancient Ruby yields,
And still a Garden by the Water blows.

6

And David's lips are lock't; but in divine
High piping Pehlevi,* with 'Wine! Wine! Wine!
    'Red Wine!' – the Nightingale cries to the Rose
That yellow Cheek of hers to incarnadine.

7

Come, fill the Cup and in the Fire of Spring
The Winter Garment of Repentance fling:
    The Bird of Time has but a little way
To fly – and Lo! the Bird is on the Wing.

8

Whether at Naishapur* or Babylon,
Whether the Cup with sweet or bitter run,
    The Wine of Life keeps oozing drop by drop,
The Leaves of Life keep falling one by one.

9

And look – a thousand Blossoms with the Day
Woke – and a thousand scatter'd into Clay:
    And this first Summer Month that brings the Rose
Shall take Jasmshyd and Kaikobad* away.

10

But come with old Khayyam, and leave the Lot
Of Kaikobad and Kaikhosru* forgot:
    Let Rustum* lay about him as he will,
Or Hatim Tai* cry Supper – heed them not.

11

With me along some Strip of Herbage strown
That just divides the desert from the sown,
    Where name of Slave and Sultan scarce is known,
And pity Sultan Mahmud* on his Throne.

12

A Book of Verses underneath the Bough,
A Jug of Wine, a Loaf of Bread – and Thou
    Beside me singing in the Wilderness –
O Wilderness were Paradise enow!

13

'How sweet is mortal Sovranty!' – think some:
Others – 'How blest the Paradise to come!'
    Ah, take the Cash in hand and waive the Rest;
O the brave Music of a *distant* Drum!

14

Look to the Rose that blows about us – 'Lo,
'Laughing,' she says, 'into the World I blow:
    'At once the silken Tassel of my Purse
'Tear, and its Treasure on the Garden throw.'

15

The Worldly Hope men set their Hearts upon
Turns Ashes – or it prospers; and anon,
    Like Snow upon the Desert's dusty Face
Lighting a little Hour or two – is gone.

16

And those who husbanded the Golden Grain,
And those who flung it to the Winds like Rain,
   Alike to no such aureate Earth are turn'd
As, buried once, Men want dug up again.

17

Were it not Folly, Spider-like* to spin
The Thread of present Life away to win –
   What? for ourselves, who know not if we shall
Breathe out the very Breath we now breathe in!*

18

Think, in this battered Caravanserai*
Whose Doorways are alternate Night and Day,
   How Sultan after Sultan with his Pomp
Abode his Hour or two, and went his way.

19

They say the Lion and the Lizard keep
The Courts where Jamshyd gloried and drank deep;
   And Bahram,* that great Hunter – the Wild Ass
Stamps o'er his Head, and he lies fast asleep.

20

I sometimes think that never blows so red
The Rose as where some buried Caesar bled;
   That every Hyacinth the Garden wears
Dropt in its Lap from some once lovely Head.

21

And this delightful Herb whose tender Green
Fledges the River's Lip on which we lean –
    Ah, lean upon it lightly! for who knows
From what once lovely Lip it springs unseen!

22

The Palace that to Heav'n his Pillars threw,
And Kings the Forehead on his Threshold drew –
    I saw the solitary Ringdove* there,
And 'Coo, coo, coo,' she cried; and 'Coo, coo, coo.'

23

Ah, my Beloved, fill the Cup that clears
TODAY of past Regrets and future Fears –
    Tomorrow? – Why, Tomorrow I may be
Myself with Yesterday's Sev'n Thousand Years.

24

Lo! some we loved, the loveliest and the best
That Time and Fate of all their Vintage prest,
    Have drunk their Cup a Round or two before,
And one by one crept silently to Rest.

25

And we, that now make merry in the Room
They left, and Summer dresses in New Bloom,
    Ourselves must we beneath the Couch of Earth
Descend, ourselves to make a Couch – for whom?

26

Ah, make the most of what we yet may spend,
Before we too into the Dust descend;
    Dust into Dust, and under Dust, to lie,
Sans Wine, sans Song, sans Singer, and – sans End!

27

Alike for those who for TODAY prepare,
And those that after some TOMORROW stare,
    A Muezzin* from the Tower of Darkness cries,
'Fools! your Reward is neither Here nor There!'

28

Why, all the Saints and Sages who discuss'd
Of the Two Worlds so learnedly, are thrust
    Like foolish Prophets forth; their Words to Scorn
Are scatter'd, and their Mouths are stopt with Dust.

29

For let Philosopher and Doctor preach
Of what they will, and what they will not – each
    Is but one Link in an eternal Chain
That none can slip, nor break, nor over-reach.

30

O come with old Khayyam, and leave the Wise
To talk; one thing is certain, that Life flies;
    One thing is certain, and the Rest is Lies;
The Flower that once has blown for ever dies.

31

Myself when young did eagerly frequent
Doctor and Saint, and heard great Argument

About it and about; but evermore
Came out by the same Door as in I went.

32

With them the Seed of Wisdom did I sow,
And with my own hand labour'd it to grow:
    And this was all the Harvest that I reap'd –
'I came like Water, and like Wind I go.'

33

Into this Universe, and *why* not knowing
Nor *whence*, like Water willy-nilly flowing:
    And out of it, as Wind along the Waste,
I know not *whither*, willy-nilly blowing.

34

What, without asking, hither hurried *whence?*
And, without asking, *whither* hurried hence!
    Another and another Cup to drown
The Memory of this Impertinence!

35

Up from Earth's Centre through the Seventh Gate
I rose, and on the Throne of Saturn sate,
    And many Knots unravel'd by the Road;
But not the Knot of Human Death and Fate.

36

There was a Door to which I found no Key:
There was a Veil past which I could not see:

Some little Talk awhile of ME and THEE
There seemed – and then no more of THEE and ME.

37

Then to the rolling Heav'n itself I cried,
Asking, 'What Lamp had Destiny to guide
   'Her little Children stumbling in the Dark?'
And – 'A blind Understanding!' Heav'n replied.

38

Earth could not answer; nor the Seas that mourn
In flowing Purple, of their Lord forlorn;
   Nor rolling Heaven, with all his Signs reveal'd
And hidden by the sleeve of Night and Morn.

39

Then to the Lip of this poor earthen Urn
I lean'd, the Secret of my Life to learn:
   And Lip to Lip it murmur'd – 'While you live,
'Drink! – for, once dead, you never shall return.'

40

I think the Vessel, that with fugitive
Articulation answer'd, once did live,
   And merry-make; and the cold Lip I kiss'd,
How many Kisses might it take – and give!

41

For in the Market-place, one Dusk of Day,
I watch'd the Potter thumping his wet Clay:

And with its all obliterated Tongue
It murmur'd – 'Gently, Brother, gently, pray!'

42

And has not such a Story from of Old
Down Man's successive Generations roll'd
    Of such a clod of saturated Earth
Cast by the Maker into Human mould?

43

Ah, fill the Cup: – what boots it to repeat
How Time is slipping underneath our Feet:
    Unborn TOMORROW, and dead YESTERDAY,
Why fret about them if TODAY be sweet!

44

And not a Drop from that our Cups we throw
For Earth to drink of, but may steal below
    To quench the Fire of Anguish in some Eye
There hidden – far beneath, and long ago.

45

As then the Tulip for her Morning sup
Of Heav'nly Vintage from the Soil looks up,
    Do you devoutly do the like, till Heav'n
To Earth invert you – like an empty Cup.

46

Perplext no more with Human or Divine
Tomorrow's Tangle to the Winds resign,

And lose your Fingers in the Tresses of
The Cypress-slender Minister of Wine.

47

And if the Wine you drink, the Lip you press,
End in the Nothing all Things end in – Yes –
    Then fancy while Thou art, Thou art but what
Thou shalt be – Nothing – Thou shalt not be less.

48

While the Rose blows along the River Brink,
With old Khayyam the Ruby Vintage drink:
    And when the Angel with his darker Draught
Draws up to Thee – take that, and do not shrink.

49

Why, if the Soul can fling the Dust aside,
And naked on the Air of Heaven ride,
    Were't not a Shame – were't not a Shame for him
In this clay carcase crippled to abide?

50

'Tis but a Tent where takes his one day's rest
A Sultan to the realm of Death addrest;
    The Sultan rises, and the dark Ferrash*
Strikes, and prepares it for another Guest.

51

And fear not lest Existence closing your
Account, and mine, should know the like no more;

The Eternal Saki* from that Bowl has pour'd
Millions of Bubbles like us, and will pour.

52

When You and I behind the Veil are past
O, but the long, long while the World shall last,
    Which of our Coming and Departure heeds
As the Sea's self should heed a Pebble-cast.

53

One Moment in Annihilation's Waste,
One Moment, of the Well of Life to taste –
    The Stars are setting and the Caravan
Starts for the Dawn of Nothing – O, make haste!

54

Would you that Spangle of Existence spend
About THE SECRET – quick about it, Friend!
    A Hair perhaps divides the False and True –
And upon what, prithee, may life depend?

55

A Hair perhaps divides the False and True;
Yes; and a single Alif* were the clue –
    Could you but find it – to the Treasure-house,
And peradventure to THE MASTER too;

56

Whose secret Presence, through Creation's veins
Running Quicksilver-like eludes your pains;

Taking all shapes from Mah* to Mahi;* and
They change and perish all – but He remains;

57

A moment guess'd – then back behind the Fold
Immerst of Darkness round the Drama roll'd
    Which, for the Pastime of Eternity,
He doth Himself contrive, enact, behold.

58

But if in vain, down on the stubborn floor
Of Earth, and up to Heav'n's unopening Door,
    You gaze TODAY, while You are You – how then
TOMORROW, You when shall be You no more?

59

How long, how long in infinite Pursuit
Of This and That endeavour and dispute?
    Better be merry with the fruitful Grape
Than sadden after none, or bitter, Fruit.

60

You know, my Friends, with what a brave Carouse
I made a Second Marriage in my House;
    Divorced old barren Reason from my Bed,
And took the Daughter of the Vine to Spouse.

61

For 'IS' and 'IS-NOT' though with Rule and Line,
And 'UP-AND-DOWN' by Logic I define,
    Of all that one should care to fathom, I
Was never deep in anything but – Wine.

62

Ah, but my Computations, People say,
Reduced the Year to better reckoning?* – Nay,
    'Twas only striking from the Calendar
Unborn Tomorrow, and dead Yesterday.

63

And lately, by the Tavern Door agape,
Came stealing through the Dusk an Angel Shape
    Bearing a Vessel on his Shoulder; and
He bid me taste of it; and 'twas – the Grape!

64

The Grape that can with Logic absolute
The Two-and-Seventy jarring Sects confute:
    The subtle Alchemist that in a Trice
Life's leaden Metal into Gold transmute.

65

The mighty Mahmud, the victorious Lord,
That all the misbelieving and black Horde
    Of Fears and Sorrows that infest the Soul
Scatters and slays with his enchanted Sword.

66

But leave the Wise to wrangle, and with me
The Quarrel of the Universe let be:
    And, in some corner of the Hubbub coucht,
Make Game of that which makes as much of Thee.

67

Why, be this Juice the growth of God, who dare
Blaspheme the twisted Tendril as a Snare?
    A Blessing, we should use it, should we not?
And if a Curse – why, then, Who set it there?

68

I must abjure the Balm of Life, I must,
Scared by some After-reckoning ta'en on trust,
    Or lured with Hope of some Diviner Drink,
To fill the Cup – when crumbled into Dust!

69

Strange, is it not? that of the Myriads who
Before us pass'd the door of Darkness through
    Not one returns to tell us of the Road,
Which to discover we must travel too.

70

The Revelations of Devout and Learn'd
Who rose before us, and as Prophets burn'd,
    Are all but Stories, which, awoke from Sleep
They told their Comrades, and to Sleep return'd.

71

I sent my Soul through the Invisible,
Some letter of that After-life to spell:
    And by and by my Soul return'd to me,
And answer'd 'I Myself am Heav'n and Hell':

72

Heav'n but the Vision of fulfill'd Desire,
And Hell the Shadow from a Soul on fire,
    Cast on the Darkness into which Ourselves
So late emerged from, shall so soon expire.

73

For in and out, above, about, below,
'Tis nothing but a Magic Shadow-show
    Played in a Box whose Candle is the Sun,
Round which we Phantom figures come and go.

74

'Tis all a Chequer-board of Nights and Days
Where Destiny with Men for Pieces plays:
    Hither and thither moves, and mates, and slays,
And one by one back in the Closet lays.

75

The Ball* no Question makes of Ayes and Noes,
But Right or Left as strikes the Player goes;
    And He that toss'd Thee down into the Field,
He knows about it all – HE knows – HE knows!

76

The Moving Finger writes; and, having writ,
Moves on: nor all thy Piety nor Wit
    Shall lure it back to cancel half a Line,
Nor all thy Tears wash out a Word of it.

77

And that inverted Bowl we call The Sky,
Whereunder crawling coop't we live and die,
    Lift not thy hands to *It* for help – for It
Rolls impotently on as Thou or I.

78

With Earth's first Clay They did the Last Man's knead,
And then of the Last Harvest sow'd the Seed:
    Yea, the first Morning of Creation wrote
What the Last Dawn of Reckoning shall read.

79

YESTERDAY *This* Day's Madness did prepare;
TOMORROW's Silence, Triumph, or Despair:
    Drink! for you know not whence you came, nor why:
Drink! for you know not why you go, nor where.

80

I tell Thee this – When, starting from the Goal,
Over the Shoulders of the flaming Foal
    Of Heav'n Parwin* and Mushtara* they flung,
In my predestin'd Plot of Dust and Soul

81

The Vine had struck a Fibre; which about
If clings my Being – let the Sufi* flout;
    Of my Base Metal may be filed a Key,
That shall unlock the Door he howls without.

82

And this I know: whether the one True Light
Kindle to Love, or Wrath consume me quite,

One Flash of it within the Tavern caught
Better than in the Temple lost outright.

83

What! out of sensless Nothing to provoke
A conscious Something to resent the Yoke
    Of unpermitted Pleasure, under pain
Of Everlasting Penalties, if broke!

84

What! from his helpless Creature be repaid
Pure Gold for what he lent him dross-allay'd –
    Sue for a Debt he never did contract,
And cannot answer – O the sorry trade!

85

O Thou, who didst with Pitfall and with Gin
Beset the Road I was to wander in,
    Thou wilt not with Predestination round
Enmesh me, and impute my Fall to Sin?

86

O Thou, who Man of baser Earth didst make,
And who with Eden didst devise the Snake;
    For all the Sin wherewith the Face of Man
Is blacken'd, Man's Forgiveness give – and take!

KUZA-NAMA* ('Book of Pots')

87

Listen again. One Evening at the Close
Of Ramazan,* ere the better Moon arose,

In that old Potter's Shop I stood alone
With the clay Population round in Rows.

88

And, strange to tell, among that Earthen Lot
Some could articulate, while others not:
    And suddenly one more impatient cried –
'Who *is* the Potter, pray, and who the Pot?'

89

Then said another – 'Surely not in vain
'My Substance from the common Earth was ta'en,
    'That He who subtly wrought me into Shape
'Should stamp me back to common Earth again.'

90

Another said – 'Why, ne'er a peevish Boy
'Would break the Bowl from which he drank in Joy;
    'Shall He that Made the Vessel in pure Love
'And Fancy, in an after Rage destroy!'

91

None answer'd this; but after Silence spake
A Vessel of a more ungainly Make:
    'They sneer at me for leaning all awry;
'What! did the Hand then of the Potter shake?'

92

Said one – 'Folks of a surly Tapster tell,
'And daub his Visage with the Smoke of Hell;

'They talk of some strict Testing of us – Pish!
'He's a Good Fellow, and 'twill all be well.'

93

Then said another with a long-drawn Sigh,
'My Clay with long oblivion is gone dry:
   'But, fill me with the old familiar Juice,
'Methinks I might recover by-and-bye!'

94

So while the Vessels one by one were speaking,
One spied the little Crescent* all were seeking:
   And then they jogg'd each other, 'Brother! Brother!
'Hark to the Porter's Shoulder-knot a-creaking!'

****

95

Ah, with the Grape my fading Life provide,
And wash my Body whence the Life has died,
   And in the Windingsheet of Vine-leaf wrapt,
So bury me by some sweet Garden-side.

96

That ev'n my buried Ashes such a Snare
Of Perfume shall fling up into the Air,
   As not a True Believer passing by
But shall be overtaken unaware.

97

Indeed the Idols I have loved so long
Have done my Credit in Men's Eye much wrong:

Have drown'd my Honour in a shallow Cup
And sold my Reputation for a Song.

98

Indeed, indeed, Repentance oft before
I swore – but was I sober when I swore?
    And then and then came Spring, and Rose-in-hand
My threadbare Penitence apieces tore.

99

And much as Wine has play'd the Infidel,
And robb'd me of my Robe of Honour – well,
    I often wonder what the Vintners buy
One half so precious as the Goods they sell.

100

Alas, that Spring should vanish with the Rose!
That Youth's sweet-scented Manuscript should close!
    The Nightingale that in the Branches sang,
Ah, whence, and whither flown again, who knows!

101

Would but the Desert of the Fountain yield
One glimpse – if dimly, yet indeed, reveal'd,
    To which the fainting Traveller might spring,
As springs the trampled Herbage of the field!

102

Would but some wingéd Angel ere too late
Arrest the yet unfolded Roll of Fate,
    And make the stern Recorder otherwise
Enregister, or quite obliterate!

103

Ah Love! could thou and I with Fate conspire
To grasp this sorry Scheme of Things entire,
    Would we not shatter it to bits – and then
Re-mould it nearer to the Heart's Desire!

104

Ah, Moon of my Delight who know'st no wane,
The Moon of Heav'n is rising once again:
    How oft hereafter rising shall she look
Through this same Garden after me – in vain!

105

And when Thyself with shining Foot shall pass
Among the Guests Star-scatter'd on the Grass,
    And in thy joyous Errand reach the Spot
Where I made one* – turn down an empty Glass!

TAMAM SHUD (*It is completed*)

Bird Parliament

Once on a time from all the Circles seven   1
Between the stedfast Earth and rolling Heaven
THE BIRDS, of all Note, Plumage, and Degree,
That float in Air, and roost upon the Tree;
And they that from the Waters snatch their Meat,
And they that scour the Desert with long Feet;
Birds of all Natures, known or not to Man,
Flock'd from all Quarters into full Divan,
On no less solemn business than to find   ⎫
Or choose, a Sultan Khalif* of their kind,   ⎬   10
For whom, if never theirs, or lost, they pined. ⎭
The Snake had his, 'twas said; and so the Beast
His Lion-lord: and Man had his, at least:
And that the Birds, who nearest were the Skies,
And went apparell'd in its Angel Dyes,
Should be without – under no better Law
Than that which lost all other in the Maw –
Disperst without a Bond of Union – nay,
Or meeting to make each the other's Prey –
This was the Grievance – this the solemn Thing   20
On which the scatter'd Commonwealth of Wing,
From all the four Winds, flying like to Cloud
That met and blacken'd Heav'n, and Thunder-loud
With Sound of whirring Wings and Beaks that clash'd
Down like a Torrent on the Desert dash'd:
Till by Degrees, the Hubbub and Pell-mell
Into some Order and Precedence fell,
And, Proclamation made of Silence, each
In special Accent, but in general Speech
That all should understand, as seem'd him best,   30
The Congregation of all Wings addrest.

And first, with Heart so full as from his Eyes
Ran weeping, up rose Tajidar* the Wise;
The mystic Mark upon whose Bosom show'd

That He alone of all the Birds THE ROAD
Had travell'd: and the Crown upon his Head
Had reach'd the Goal; and He stood forth and said:

'O Birds, by what Authority divine
I speak you know by *His* authentic Sign,
And Name, emblazon'd on my Breast and Bill: 40
Whose Counsel I assist at, and fulfil:
At His Behest I measured as he plann'd
The Spaces of the Air and Sea and Land;
I gauged the secret sources of the Springs
From Cloud to Fish:* the Shadow of my Wings
Dream'd over sleeping Deluge: piloted   ⎫
The Blast that bore Sulayman's* Throne: and led   ⎬
The Cloud of Birds that canopied his Head;   ⎭
Whose Word I brought to Balkis: and I shared
The Counsel that with Asaf he prepared.   50
And now *you* want a Khalif: and I know
Him, and his whereabout, and How to go:
And go alone I could, and plead your cause
Alone for all: but, by the eternal laws,
Yourselves by Toil and Travel of your own
Must for your old Delinquency atone.
Were you indeed not blinded by the Curse
Of Self-exile, that still grows worse and worse,
Yourselves would know that, though *you* see him not,
He *is* with you this Moment, on this Spot,   60
Your Lord through all Forgetfulness and Crime,
Here, There, and Everywhere, and through all Time.
But as a Father, whom some wayward Child
By sinful Self-will has unreconciled,
Waits till the sullen Reprobate at cost
Of long Repentance should regain the Lost;
Therefore, yourselves to see as you are seen,
Yourselves must bridge the Gulf you made between
By such a Search and Travel to be gone

Up to the mighty mountain Kaf, whereon 70
Hinges the World, and round about whose Knees
Into one Ocean mingle the Sev'n Seas;
In whose impenetrable Forest-folds
Of Light and Dark "Symurgh"* his Presence holds;
Not to be reach'd, if to be reach'd at all
But by a Road the stoutest might apal;
Of Travel not of Days or Months, but Years –
Life-long perhaps: of Dangers, Doubts, and Fears
As yet unheard of: Sweat of Blood and Brain ⎫
Interminable – often all in vain – ⎬ 80
And, if successful, no Return again: ⎭
A Road whose very Preparation scared
The Traveller who yet must be prepared.
Who then this Travel to Result would bring
Needs both a Lion's Heart beneath the Wing,
And even more, a Spirit purified
Of Worldly Passion, Malice, Lust, and Pride:
Yea, ev'n of Worldly *Wisdom*, which grows dim
And dark, the nearer it approaches *Him*,
Who to the Spirit's Eye alone reveal'd, 90
By sacrifice of Wisdom's self unseal'd;
Without which none who reach the Place could bear
To look upon the Glory dwelling there.'

One Night from out the swarming City Gate
Stept holy Bajazyd, to meditate
Alone amid the breathing Fields that lay ⎫
In solitary Silence leagues away, ⎬
Beneath a Moon and Stars as bright as Day. ⎭
And the Saint wondering such a Temple were,
And so lit up, and scarce one worshipper, 100
A voice from Heav'n amid the stillness said:
'The Royal Road is not for all to tread,
Nor is the Royal Palace for the Rout,

Who, even if they reach it, are shut out.
The Blaze that from my Harim window breaks
With fright the Rabble of the Roadside takes;
And ev'n of those that at my Portal din,
Thousands may knock for one that enters in.'

———————

Thus spoke the Tajidar: and the wing'd Crowd,
That underneath his Word in Silence bow'd,   110
Clapp'd Acclamation: and their Hearts and Eyes
Were kindled by the Firebrand of the Wise.
They felt their Degradation: they believed
The word that told them how to be retrieved,
And in that glorious Consummation won
Forgot the Cost at which it must be done.
'They only *long'd* to follow: they would go
Whither he led, through Flood, or Fire, or Snow' –
So cried the Multitude. But some there were
Who listen'd with a cold disdainful air,   120
Content with what they were, or grudging Cost
Of Time or Travel that might all be lost;
These, one by one, came forward, and preferr'd
Unwise Objection: which the wiser Word
Shot with direct Reproof, or subtly round
With Argument and Allegory wound.

The Pheasant first would know by what pretence
The Tajidar to that pre-eminence
Was raised – a Bird, but for his lofty Crest
(And such the Pheasant had) like all the Rest –   130
Who answer'd – 'By no Virtue of my own
Sulayman chose me, but by *His* alone:
Not by the Gold and Silver of my Sighs
Made mine, but the free Largess of his Eyes.
Behold the Grace of Allah comes and goes

As to Itself is good: and no one knows
Which way it turns: in that mysterious Court
Not he most finds who furthest travels for't.
For one may crawl upon his knees Life-long,
And yet may never reach, or all go wrong: 140
Another just arriving at the Place
He toil'd for, and – the Door shut in his Face:
Whereas Another, scarcely gone a Stride,
And suddenly – Behold he is Inside! –
But though the Runner win not, he that *stands*,
No Thorn will turn to Roses in *his* Hands:
Each one must do his best and all endure,
And all endeavour, hoping but not sure.
Heav'n its own Umpire is; its Bidding do,
And Thou perchance shalt be Sulayman's too.'   150

One day Shah Mahmud,* riding with the Wind
A-hunting, left his Retinue behind,
And coming to a River, whose swift Course
Doubled back Game and Dog, and Man and Horse,
Beheld upon the Shore a little Lad
A-fishing, very poor, and Tatter-clad
He was, and weeping as his Heart would break.
So the Great Sultan, for good humour's sake
Pull'd in his Horse a moment, and drew nigh,
And after making his Salam,* ask'd why   160
He wept – weeping, the Sultan said, so sore
As he had never seen one weep before.
The Boy look'd up, and 'O Amir,'* he said,   ⎫
'Sev'n of us are at home, and Father dead,   ⎬
And Mother left with scarce a Bit of Bread: ⎭
And now since Sunrise have I fish'd – and see!
Caught nothing for our Supper – Woe is Me!'
The Sultan lighted from his horse. 'Behold,'

Said he, 'Good Fortune will not be controll'd:
And, since Today yours seems to turn from you,   170
Suppose we try for once what mine will do,
And we will share alike in all I win.'
So the Shah took, and flung his Fortune in,
The Net; which, cast by the Great Mahmud's Hand,
A hundred glittering Fishes brought to Land.
The Lad look'd up in Wonder – Mahmud smiled
And vaulted into Saddle. But the Child
Ran after – 'Nay, Amir, but half the Haul
Is yours by Bargain' – 'Nay, Today take all,'
The Sultan cried, and shook his Bridle free –   180
'But mind – Tomorrow All belongs to Me –'
And so rode off. Next morning at Divan
The Sultan's Mind upon his Bargain ran,
And being somewhat in a mind for sport
Sent for the Lad: who, carried up to Court,
And marching into Royalty's full Blaze
With such a Catch of Fish as yesterday's,
The Sultan call'd and set him by his side,
And asking him, 'What Luck?' The Boy replied,
'*This* is the Luck that follows every Cast,   190
Since o'er my Net the Sultan's Shadow pass'd.'

———

Then came *The Nightingale*, from such a Draught
Of Ecstasy that from the Rose he quaff'd
Reeling as drunk, and ever did distil
In exquisite divisions from his Bill
To inflame the Hearts of Men – and thus sang He –
'To me alone, alone, is giv'n the Key
Of Love; of whose whole Mystery possesst,
When I reveal a little to the Rest,
Forthwith Creation listening forsakes   200
The Reins of Reason, and my Frenzy takes:

Yea, whosoever once has quaff'd this wine
He leaves unlisten'd David's Song for mine.
In vain do Men for my Divisions strive,
And die themselves making dead Lutes alive:
I hang the Stars with Meshes for Men's Souls:
The Garden underneath my Music rolls.
The long, long Morns that mourn the Rose away
I sit in silence, and on Anguish prey:
But the first Air which the New Year shall breathe   210
Up to my Boughs of Message from beneath
That in her green Harim my Bride unveils,
My Throat bursts silence and *her* Advent hails,
Who in her crimson Volume registers
The Notes of Him whose Life is lost in hers.*
The Rose I love and worship now is here;
If dying, yet reviving, Year by Year;
But that you tell of, all my Life why waste
In vainly searching; or, if found, not taste?'

So with Division infinite and Trill   220
On would the Nightingale have warbled still,
And all the World have listen'd; but a Note
Of sterner Import check'd the lovesick Throat.

'O watering with thy melodious Tears
Love's Garden, and who dost indeed the Ears
Of men with thy melodious Fingers mould
As David's Finger Iron did of old:*
Why not, like David, dedicate thy Dower
Of Song to something better than a Flower?
Empress indeed of Beauty, so they say,   230
But one whose Empire hardly lasts a Day,
By Insurrection of the Morning's Breath
That made her hurried to Decay and Death:
And while she lasts contented to be seen,
And worshipt, for the Garden's only Queen,

Leaving thee singing on thy Bough forlorn,
Or if she smile on Thee, perhaps in Scorn.'

———————

Like that fond Dervish waiting in the throng
When some World-famous Beauty went along,
Who smiling on the Antic as she pass'd –   240
Forthwith Staff, Bead and Scrip away he cast,
And grovelling in the Kennel, took to whine
Before her Door among the Dogs and Swine.
Which when she often went unheeding by,
But one day quite as heedless ask'd him – 'Why?' –
He told of that one Smile, which, all the Rest
Passing, had kindled Hope within his Breast –
Again she smiled and said, 'O self-beguiled
Poor Wretch, *at* whom and not *on* whom I smiled.'

═══════

Then came the subtle *Parrot* in a coat   250
Greener than Greensward, and about his Throat
A Collar ran of sub-sulphureous Gold;
And in his Beak a Sugar-plum he troll'd,
That all his Words with luscious Lisping ran,
And to this Tune – 'O cruel Cage, and Man
More iron still who did confine me there,
Who else with him* whose Livery I wear
Ere this to his Eternal Fount had been,
And drunk what should have kept me ever-green.
But now I know the Place, and I am free   260
To go, and all the Wise will follow Me.
Some' – and upon the Nightingale one Eye
He leer'd – 'for nothing but the Blossom sigh:
But I am for the luscious Pulp that grows
Where, and for which the Blossom only blows:

And which so long as the Green Tree provides
What better grows along Kaf's dreary Sides?
And what more needful Prophet *there* than He
Who gives me Life to nip it from the Tree?'

To whom the Tajidar – 'O thou whose Best   270
In the green leaf of Paradise is drest,
But whose Neck kindles with a lower Fire –
O slip the collar off of base Desire,
And stand apparell'd in Heav'n's Woof entire!*
This Life that hangs so sweet about your Lips
But, spite of all your Khizar, slips and slips,
What is it but itself the coarser Rind
Of the True Life withinside and behind,
Which he shall never never reach unto
Till the gross Shell of Carcase he break through?'   280

For what said He, that dying Hermit, whom
Your Prophet came to, trailing through the Gloom
His Emerald Vest, and tempted – 'Come with Me,
And Live.' The Hermit answered – 'Not with Thee.
Two Worlds there are, and *This* was thy Design,
And thou hast got it; but *The Next* is mine;
Whose Fount is *this* life's Death, and to whose Side
Ev'n now I find my Way without a Guide.'

Then like a Sultan glittering in all Rays
Of Jewelry, and deckt with his own Blaze,   290
The glorious *Peacock* swept into the Ring:
And, turning slowly that the glorious Thing
Might fill all Eyes with wonder, thus said He.
'Behold, the Secret Artist, making me,

With no one Colour of the skies bedeckt,
But from its Angel's Feathers did select
To make up mine withal, the Gabriel
Of all the Birds: though from my Place I fell
In Eden, when Acquaintance I did make
In those blest days with that Sev'n-headed Snake,*   300
And thence with him, my perfect Beauty marr'd
With these ill Feet, was thrust out and debarr'd.
Little I care for Worldly Fruit or Flower,
Would you restore me to lost Eden's Bower,
But first my Beauty making all complete
With reparation of these ugly Feet.'

'Were it,' 'twas answer'd, 'only to return
To that lost Eden, better far to burn
In Self-abasement up thy pluméd Pride,
And ev'n with lamer feet to creep inside –   310
But all mistaken you and all like you
That long for that lost Eden as the true;
Fair as it was, still nothing but the shade
And Out-court of the Majesty that made.
That which I point you tow'rd, and which the King
I tell you of broods over with his Wing,
With no deciduous leaf, but with the Rose
Of Spiritual Beauty, smells and glows:
No plot of Earthly Pleasance, but the whole
True Garden of the Universal Soul.'   320

————————

For so Creation's Master-Jewel fell
From that same Eden: loving which too well,
The Work before the Artist did prefer,
And in the Garden lost the Gardener.
Wherefore one Day about the Garden went
A voice that found him in his false Content,

And like a bitter Sarsar of the North*
Shrivell'd the Garden up, and drove him forth
Into the Wilderness: and so the Eye
Of Eden closed on him till by and by.   330

———————

Then from a Ruin where conceal'd he lay
Watching his buried Gold, and hating Day,
Hooted *The Owl.* – 'I tell you, my Delight
Is in the Ruin and the Dead of Night
Where I was born, and where I love to wone
All my Life long, sitting on some cold stone
Away from all your roystering Companies,
In some dark Corner where a Treasure lies;
That, buried by some Miser in the Dark,
Speaks up to me at Midnight like a Spark;   340
And o'er it like a Talisman I brood,
Companion of the Serpent and the Toad.
What need of other Sovereign, having found,
And keeping as in Prison underground,
One before whom all other Kings bow down,
And with his glittering Heel their Foreheads crown?'

'He that a Miser lives and Miser dies,
At the Last Day what Figure shall he rise?'

———————

A Fellow all his life lived hoarding Gold,
And, dying, hoarded left it. And behold,   350
One Night his Son saw peering through the House
A Man, with yet the semblance of a Mouse,
Watching a crevice in the Wall – and cried –
'My Father?' – 'Yes,' the Musulman replied,
'Thy Father!' – 'But why watching thus?' – 'For fear

Lest any smell my Treasure buried here.'
'But wherefore, Sir, so metamousified?'
'Because, my Son, such is the true outside }
Of the inner Soul by which I lived and died.' }

⸻

'Aye,' said *The Partridge*, with his Foot and Bill   360
Crimson with raking Rubies from the Hill,
And clattering his Spurs – 'Wherewith the Ground
I stab,' said he, 'for Rubies, that, when found
I swallow; which, as soon as swallow'd, turn
To Sparks which though my beak and eyes do burn.
Gold, as you say, is but dull Metal dead,
And hanging on the Hoarder's Soul like Lead:
But Rubies that have Blood within, and grown
And nourisht in the Mountain Heart of Stone,
Burn with an inward Light, which they inspire,   370
And make their Owners Lords of their Desire.'

To whom the Tajidar – 'As idly sold
To the quick Pebble as the drowsy Gold,
As dead when sleeping in their mountain mine
As dangerous to Him who makes them shine:
Slavish indeed to do their Lord's Commands,
And slave-like aptest to escape his Hands,
And serve a second Master like the first,
And working all their wonders for the worst.'

⸻

Never was Jewel after or before   380
Like that Sulayman for a Signet wore:
Whereby one Ruby, weighing scarce a grain
Did Sea and Land and all therein constrain,
Yea, ev'n the Winds of Heav'n – made the fierce East

Bear his League-wide Pavilion like a Beast,
Whither he would: yea, the Good Angel held
His subject, and the lower Fiend compell'd.
Till, looking round about him in his pride,
He overtax'd the Fountain that supplied,
Praying that after him no Son of Clay   390
Should ever touch his Glory. And one Day
Almighty God his Jewel stole away,
And gave it to the Div, who with the Ring
Wore also the Resemblance of the King,
And so for forty days play'd such a Game
As blots Sulayman's forty years with Shame.

———————

Then *The Shah-Falcon*, tossing up his Head
Blink-hooded as it was – 'Behold,' he said,
'I am the chosen Comrade of the King,
And perch upon the Fist that wears the Ring;   400
Born, bred, and nourisht, in the Royal Court,
I take the Royal Name and make the Sport.
And if strict Discipline I undergo
And half my Life am blinded – be it so;
Because the Shah's Companion ill may brook
On aught save Royal Company to look.
And why am I to leave my King, and fare
With all these Rabble Wings I know not where?' –

'O blind indeed' – the Answer was, 'and dark
To any but a vulgar Mortal Mark,   410
And drunk with Pride of Vassalage to those
Whose Humour like their Kingdom comes and goes;
All Mutability: who one Day please
To give: and next Day what they gave not seize:
Like to the Fire: a dangerous Friend at best,
Which who keeps farthest from does wiseliest.'

A certain Shah there was in Days foregone
Who had a lovely Slave he doted on,
And cherish'd as the Apple of his Eye,
Clad gloriously, fed sumptuously, set high,   420
And never was at Ease were *He* not by,
Who yet, for all this Sunshine, Day by Day
Was seen to wither like a Flower away.
Which, when observing, one without the Veil
Of Favour ask'd the Favourite – 'Why so pale
And sad?' thus sadly answer'd the poor Thing –
'No Sun that rises sets until the King,
Whose Archery is famous among Men,
Aims at an Apple on my Head,* and when
The stricken Apple splits, and those who stand   430
Around cry "Lo! the Shah's unerring Hand!"
Then He too laughing asks me "Why so pale
And sorrow-some? as could the Sultan fail,
Who such a master of the Bow confest,
And aiming by the Head that he loves best."'

Then on a sudden swoop'd *The Phœnix* down
As though he wore as well as gave The Crown:*
And cried – 'I care not, I, to wait on Kings,
Whose crowns are but the Shadow of my Wings!'

'Aye,' was the Answer – 'And, pray, how has sped,   440
On which it lighted, many a mortal Head?'

A certain Sultan dying, his Vizier
In Dream beheld him, and in mortal Fear

Began – 'O mighty Shah of Shahs! Thrice-blest' –
But loud the Vision shriek'd and struck its Breast,
And 'Stab me not with empty Title!' cried –
'One only Shah there is, and none beside,
Who from his Throne above for certain Ends
Awhile some Spangle of his Glory lends
To Men on Earth; but calling in again   450
Exacts a strict account of every Grain.
Sultan I lived, and held the World in scorn: ⎫
O better had I glean'd the Field of Corn!   ⎬
O better had I been a Beggar born,   ⎭
And for my Throne and Crown, down in the Dust
My living Head had laid where Dead I must!
O wither'd, wither'd, wither'd, be the Wing
Whose overcasting Shadow made me King!'

Then from a Pond, where all day long he kept,
Waddled the dapper *Duck* demure, adept   460
At infinite Ablution, and precise
In keeping of his Raiment clean and nice.
And 'Sure of all the Race of Birds,' said He,
'None for Religious Purity like Me,
Beyond what strictest Rituals prescribe –
Methinks I am the Saint of all our Tribe,
To whom, by Miracle, the Water, that
I wash in, also makes my Praying-Mat.'

To whom, more angrily than all, replied
The Leader, lashing that religious Pride,   470
That under ritual Obedience
To outer Law with inner might dispense:
For, fair as all the Feather to be seen,
Could one see *through*, the Maw was not so clean:
But He that made both Maw and Feather too

Would take account of, seeing through and through.

———————

A Shah returning to his Capital,
His subjects drest it forth in Festival,
Thronging with Acclamation Square and Street,
And kneeling flung before his Horse's feet   480
Jewel and Gold. All which with scarce an Eye
The Sultan superciliously rode by:
Till coming to the public Prison, They
Who dwelt within those grisly Walls, by way
Of Welcome, having neither Pearl nor Gold,
Over the wall chopt Head and Carcase roll'd,
Some almost parcht to Mummy with the Sun,
Some wet with Execution that day done.
At which grim Compliment at last the Shah
Drew Bridle: and amid a wild Hurrah   490
Of savage Recognition, smiling threw
Silver and Gold among the wretched Crew,
And so rode forward. Whereat of his Train
One wondering that, while others sued in vain
With costly gifts, which carelessly he pass'd,
But smiled at ghastly Welcome like the last;
The Shah made answer – 'All that Pearl and Gold
Of ostentatious Welcome only told:
A little with great Clamour from the Store
Of hypocrites who kept at home much more.   500
But when those sever'd Heads and Trunks I saw –
Save by strict Execution of my Law
They had not parted company; not one
But told my Will not talk'd about, but *done*.'

———————

Then from a Wood was heard unseen to coo

The Ring-dove – 'Yúsuf!* Yúsuf! Yúsuf! Yú-'
(For thus her sorrow broke her Note in twain,
And, just where broken, took it up again)
'-suf! Yúsuf! Yúsuf! Yúsuf!' – But one Note,
Which still repeating, she made hoarse her throat: 510

Till checkt – 'O You, who with your idle Sighs
Block up the Road of better Enterprise;
Sham Sorrow all, or bad as sham if true,
When once the better thing is come to *do*;
Beware lest wailing thus you meet *his* Doom
Who all too long his Darling wept, from whom
You draw the very Name you hold so dear,
And which the World is somewhat tired to hear.'

<hr>

When Yusuf from his Father's Home was torn,
The Patriarch's Heart was utterly forlorn,   520
And, like a Pipe with but one stop, his Tongue
With nothing but the name of 'Yusuf' rung.
Then down from Heaven's Branches flew the *Bird
Of Heav'n** and said 'God wearies of that word:
Hast thou not else to do and else to say?'
So Jacob's lips were sealéd from that Day.
But one Night in a Vision, far away
His darling in some alien Field he saw
Binding the Sheaf; and what between the Awe
Of God's Displeasure and the bitter Pass   530
Of passionate Affection, sigh'd 'Alas –'
And stopp'd – But with the morning Sword of Flame
That oped his Eyes the sterner Angel's came –
'For the forbidden Word not utter'd by
Thy Lips was yet sequester'd in that Sigh.'
And the right Passion whose Excess was wrong
Blinded the aged Eyes that wept too long.

And after these came others – arguing,
Enquiring and excusing – some one Thing,
And some another – endless to repeat,   540
But, in the Main, Sloth, Folly, or Deceit.
Their Souls were to the vulgar Figure cast
Of earthly Victual not of Heavenly Fast.
At last one smaller Bird, of a rare kind,
Of modest Plume and unpresumptuous Mind,
Whisper'd 'O Tajidar, we know indeed
How Thou both knowest, and would'st help our Need;
For thou art wise and holy, and hast been
Behind the Veil, and there *The Presence* seen.
But we are weak and vain, with little care   550
Beyond our yearly Nests and daily Fare –
How should we reach the Mountain? and if there
How get so great a Prince to hear our Prayer?
For there, you say, dwells *The Symurgh* alone
In Glory, like Sulayman on his Throne,
And we but Pismires at his feet: can He
Such puny Creatures stoop to hear, or see;
Or hearing, seeing, *own* us – unakin
As He to Folly, Woe, and Death, and Sin?' –

To whom the Tajidar, whose Voice for those   560
Bewilder'd ones to full Compassion rose –
'O lost so long in exile, you disclaim
The very Fount of Being whence you came,
Cannot be parted from, and, will or no,
Whether for Good or Evil must re-flow!
For look – the Shadows into which the Light
Of his pure Essence down by infinite
Gradation dwindles, which at random play
Through Space in Shape indefinite – one Ray
Of his Creative *Will* into *defined*   570

Creation quickens: We that swim the Wind,
And they the Flood below, and Man and Beast
That walk between, from Lion to the least
Pismire that creeps along Sulayman's Wall –
Yea, that in which they swim, fly, walk, and crawl –
However near the Fountain Light, or far
Removed, yet *His* authentic Shadows are;
Dead Matter's Self but the dark Residue
Exterminating Glory dwindles to.
A Mystery too fearful in the Crowd   580
To utter – scarcely to Thyself aloud –
But when in solitary Watch and Prayer
Consider'd: and religiously beware
Lest Thou the Copy with the Type confound;
And *Deity*, with Deity indrown'd, –
For as pure Water into purer Wine
Incorporating shall itself refine
While the dull Drug lies half-resolved below,
With Him and with his Shadows is it so:
The baser Forms, to whatsoever Change   590
Subject, still vary through their lower Range:
To which the *higher* even shall decay,
That, letting ooze their better Part away
For Things of Sense and Matter, in the End
Shall merge into the Clay to which they tend.
Unlike to him, who straining through the Bond
Of outward Being for a Life beyond,
While the gross Worldling to *his* Centre clings, ⎫
That draws him deeper in, exulting springs   ⎬
To merge him in the central *Soul* of Things. ⎭   600
And shall not he pass home with other Zest
Who, with full Knowledge, yearns for such a Rest,
Than he, who with his better self at strife,
Drags on the weary Exile call'd *This Life?* –
One, like a child with outstretcht Arms and Face
Upturn'd, anticipates his Sire's Embrace;
The other crouching like a guilty Slave

Till flogg'd to Punishment across the Grave.
And, knowing that *His* glory ill can bear
The unpurged Eye; do thou Thy Breast prepare;   610
And the mysterious Mirror He set there,
To temper his reflected Image in,
Clear of Distortion, Doubleness, and Sin:
And in thy Conscience understanding *this*,
The *Double* only *seems*, but The *One is*,
Thyself to Self-annihilation give
That this false *Two* in that true *One* may live.
For this I say: if, looking in thy Heart,
Thou for *Self-whole* mistake thy *Shadow-part*,
That Shadow-part indeed into *The Sun*   620
Shall melt, but senseless of its Union:
But in that Mirror if with purgéd eyes
Thy Shadow Thou *for* Shadow recognise,
Then shalt Thou back into thy Centre fall
A conscious Ray of that eternal *All*.'

He ceased, and for awhile Amazement quell'd
The Host, and in the Chain of Silence held:
A Mystery so awful who would dare –
So glorious who would not wish – to share?
So Silence brooded on the feather'd Folk,   630
Till here and there a timid Murmur broke
From some too poor in honest Confidence,
And then from others of too much Pretence;
Whom both, as each unduly hoped or fear'd,
The Tajidar in answer check'd or cheer'd.

Some said their Hearts were good indeed to go
The Way he pointed out: but they were slow
Of Comprehension, and scarce understood
Their present Evil or the promised Good:
And so, tho' willing to do all they could,   640
Must not they fall short, or go wholly wrong,
On such mysterious Errand, and so long?

Whom the wise Leader bid but Do their Best
In Hope and Faith, and leave to *Him* the rest,
For He who fix'd the Race, and knew its Length
And Danger, also knew the Runner's Strength.

———————

Shah Mahmud, absent on an Enterprise,
Ayas, the very Darling of his eyes,
At home under an Evil Eye fell sick,
Then cried the Sultan to a soldier 'Quick!   650
To Horse! to Horse! without a Moment's Stay, –
The shortest Road with all the Speed you may, –
Or, by the Lord, your Head shall pay for it!' –
Off went the Soldier, plying Spur and Bit –
Over the sandy Desert, over green
Valley, and Mountain, and the Stream between,
Without a Moment's Stop for rest or bait, –
Up to the City – to the Palace Gate –
Up to the Presence-Chamber at a Stride –
And Lo! The Sultan at his Darling's side! –   660
Then thought the Soldier – 'I have done my Best,
And yet shall die for it.' The Sultan guess'd
His Thought and smiled. 'Indeed your Best you did,
The nearest Road you knew, and well you rid:
And if *I* knew a shorter, my Excess
Of Knowledge does but justify thy Less.'

———————

And then, with drooping Crest and Feather, came
Others, bow'd down with Penitence and Shame.
They long'd indeed to go; 'but how begin,
Mesh'd and entangled as they were in Sin   670
Which often-times Repentance of past Wrong
As often broken had but knit more strong?'

Whom the wise Leader bid be of good cheer,
And, conscious of the Fault, dismiss the Fear,
Nor at the very Entrance of the Fray
Their Weapon, ev'n if broken, fling away:
Since Mercy on the broken Branch anew
Would blossom were but each Repentance true.

For did not God his Prophet take to Task?
'*Sev'n-times* of Thee did Karun Pardon ask;   680
Which, hadst thou been like Me his Maker – yea,
But present at the Kneading of his Clay
With those twain Elements of Hell and Heav'n, –
One prayer had won what Thou deny'st to Sev'n.'

For like a Child sent with a fluttering Light
To feel his way along a gusty Night
Man walks the World: again and yet again
The Lamp shall be by Fits of Passion slain:
But shall not He who sent him from the Door
Relight the Lamp once more, and yet once more?   690

———

When the rebellious Host from Death shall wake
Black with Despair of Judgment, God shall take
Ages of holy Merit from the Count
Of Angels to make up Man's short Amount,
And bid the murmuring Angel gladly spare
Of that which, undiminishing his Share
Of Bliss, shall rescue Thousands from the Cost
Of Bankruptcy within the Prison lost.

———

Another Story told how in the Scale
Good Will beyond mere Knowledge would prevail.   700

In Paradise the Angel Gabriel heard
The Lips of Allah trembling with the Word
Of perfect Acceptation: and he thought
'Some perfect Faith such perfect Answer wrought,
But whose?' – And therewith slipping from the Crypt
Of Sidra,* through the Angel-ranks he slipt
Watching what Lip yet trembled with the Shot
That so had hit the Mark – but found it not.
Then, in a Glance to Earth, he threaded through
Mosque, Palace, Cell and Cottage of the True   710
Belief – in vain; so back to Heaven went
And – Allah's Lips still trembling with assent!
Then the tenacious Angel once again
Threaded the Ranks of Heav'n and Earth – in vain –
Till, once again return'd to Paradise,
There, looking into God's, the Angel's Eyes
Beheld the Prayer that brought that Benison
Rising like Incense from the Lips of one
Who to an Idol bowed – as best he knew
Under that False God worshipping the True.   720

And then came others whom the summons found
Not wholly sick indeed, but far from sound:
Whose light inconstant Soul alternate flew
From Saint to Sinner, and to both untrue;
Who like a niggard Tailor, tried to match
Truth's single Garment with a worldly Patch.
A dangerous Game; for, striving to adjust
The hesitating Scale of either Lust,
That which had least within it upward flew,
And still the weightier to the Earth down drew,   730
And, while suspended between Rise and Fall,

Apt with a shaking Hand to forfeit all.

———————

There was a Queen of Egypt like the Bride
Of Night, Full-moon-faced and Canopus-eyed,
Whom one among the meanest of her Crowd
Loved – and she knew it (for he loved aloud),
And sent for him, and said 'Thou lov'st thy Queen:
Now therefore Thou hast this to choose between:
Fly for thy Life: or for this one night Wed
Thy Queen, and with the Sunrise lose thy Head.'   740
He paused – he turn'd to fly – she struck him dead.
'For had he truly loved his Queen,' said She,
'He would at once have giv'n his Life for me,
And Life and Wife had carried: but he lied;
And loving only Life, has justly died.'

———————

And then came one who having clear'd his Throat
With sanctimonious Sweetness in his Note
Thus lisp'd – 'Behold I languish from the first
With passionate and unrequited Thirst
Of Love for more than any mortal Bird.   750
Therefore have I withdrawn me from the Herd
To pine in Solitude. But Thou at last
Hast drawn a line across the dreary Past,
And sure I am by Foretaste that the Wine
I long'd for, and Thou tell'st of, shall be mine.'

But he was sternly checkt. 'I tell thee this:
Such Boast is no Assurance of such Bliss:
Thou canst not even fill the sail of Prayer
Unless from *Him* breathe that authentic Air
That shall lift up the Curtain that divides   760

His Lover from the Harim where *He* hides –
And the Fulfilment of thy Vows must be,
Not from thy Love for Him, but His for Thee.'

———————

The third night after Bajazyd had died,
One saw him, in a dream, at his Bedside,
And said, 'Thou Bajazyd? Tell me O Pyr,
How fared it there with Munkar and Nakyr?'*
And Bajazyd replied, 'When from the Grave
They met me rising, and "If Allah's slave"
Ask'd me, "or collar'd with the Chain of Hell?"   770
I said "Not I but God alone can tell:
My Passion for his service were but fond
Ambition had not He approved the Bond:
Had He not round my neck the Collar thrown
And told me in the Number of his own;
And that *He* only knew. What signifies
A hundred Years of Prayer if none replies?" '

———————

'But,' said Another, 'then shall none the Seal
Of Acceptation on his Forehead feel
Ere the Grave yield them on the other Side   780
Where all is settled?'

                    But the Chief replied –
'Enough for us to know that who is meet
Shall enter, and with unreprovéd Feet,
(Ev'n as he might upon the Waters walk)
The Presence-room, and in the Presence talk
With such unbridled Licence as shall seem
To the Uninitiated to blaspheme.'

Just as another Holy Spirit fled,
The Skies above him burst into a Bed
Of Angels looking down and singing clear   790
'Nightingale! Nightingale! thy Rose is here!'
And yet, the Door wide open to that Bliss,
As some hot Lover slights a scanty Kiss,
The Saint cried 'All I sigh'd for come to *this?*
I who lifelong have struggled, Lord, to be
Not of thy Angels one, but one with Thee!'

Others were sure that all he said was true:
They were extremely wicked, that they knew:
And much they long'd to go at once – but some,
They said, so unexpectedly had come   800
Leaving their Nests half-built – in bad Repair –
With Children in – Themselves about to pair –
'Might he not choose a better Season – nay,
Better perhaps a Year or Two's Delay,
Till all was settled, and themselves more stout
And strong to carry their Repentance out –
And then' –

                'And then, the same or like Excuse,
With harden'd Heart and Resolution loose
With dallying: and old Age itself engaged
Still to shirk that which shirking we have aged;   810
And so with Self-delusion, till, too late,
Death upon all Repentance shuts the Gate;
Or some fierce blow compels the Way to choose,
And forced Repentance half its Virtue lose.'

As of an aged Indian King they tell
Who, when his Empire with his Army fell
Under young Mahmud's Sword of Wrath, was sent
At sunset to the Conqueror in his Tent;
But, ere the old King's silver head could reach
The Ground, was lifted up – with kindly Speech,   820
And with so holy Mercy reassured,
That, after due Persuasion, he abjured
His idols, sate upon Mahmud's Divan,
And took the Name and Faith of Musulman.
But when the Night fell, in his Tent alone
The poor old King was heard to weep and groan
And smite his Bosom; which, when Mahmud knew,
He went to him and said 'Lo, if Thou rue
Thy lost Dominion, Thou shalt wear the Ring
Of thrice as large a Realm.' But the dark King   830
Still wept, and Ashes on his Forehead threw
And cried 'Not for my Kingdom lost I rue;
But thinking how at the Last Day, will stand
The Prophet with *The Volume* in his Hand,
And ask of me "How was't that, in thy Day
Of Glory, Thou didst turn from Me and slay
My People; but soon as thy Infidel
Before my True Believers' Army fell
Like Corn before the Reaper – thou didst own
His Sword who scoutedst *Me*." Of seed so sown   840
What profitable Harvest should be grown?'

———————

Then after cheering others who delay'd,
Not of the Road but of Themselves afraid,
The Tajidar the Troop of those address'd,
Whose uncomplying Attitude confess'd
Their Souls entangled in the old Deceit,
And hankering still after forbidden Meat –

'O ye who so long feeding on the Husk
Forgo the Fruit, and doting on the Dusk
Of the false Dawn, are blinded to the True: 850
That in the Maidan* of this World pursue
The Golden Ball which, driven to the Goal,
Wins the World's Game* but loses your own Soul:
Or like to Children after Bubbles run
That still elude your Fingers; or, if won,
Burst in Derision at your Touch; all thin
Glitter without, and empty Wind within.
So as a prosperous Worldling on the Bed
Of Death – "Behold, I am as one," he said,
"Who all my Life long have been measuring Wind,   860
And, dying, now leave even that behind" –
This World's a Nest in which the Cockatrice
Is warm'd and hatcht of Vanity and Vice:
A false Bazaar whose Wares are all a lie,
Or never worth the Price at which you buy:
A many-headed Monster that, supplied
The faster, faster is unsatisfied;
So as one, hearing a rich Fool one day
To God for yet one other Blessing pray,
Bid him no longer bounteous Heaven tire   870
For Life to feed, but Death to quench, the Fire.
And what are all the Vanities and Wiles
In which the false World decks herself and smiles
To draw Men down into her harlot Lap?
Lusts of the Flesh that Soul and Body sap,
And, melting Soul down into carnal Lust,
Ev'n that for which 'tis sacrificed disgust:
Or Lust of worldly Glory – hollow more
Than the Drum beaten at the Sultan's Door,
And fluctuating with the Breath of Man   880
As the Vain Banner flapping in the Van.
And Lust of Gold – perhaps of Lusts the worst;
The mis-created Idol most accurst
That between Man and Him who made him stands:

The Felon that with suicidal hands
He sweats to dig and rescue from his Grave,
And sets at large to make Himself its Slave.

'For lo, to what worse than oblivion gone
Are some the cozening World most doted on.
Pharaoh tried *Glory*: and his Chariots drown'd: 890
Karun with all his Gold went underground:
Down toppled Nembroth* with his airy Stair:
Schedad among his Roses lived – but *where?*

'And as the World upon her victims feeds
So She herself goes down the Way she leads.
For all her false allurements are the Threads
The Spider* from her Entrail spins, and spreads
For Home and hunting-ground: And by and by
Darts at due Signal on the tangled Fly,
Seizes, dis-wings, and drains the Life, and leaves   900
The swinging Carcase, and forthwith re-weaves
Her Web: each Victim adding to the store
Of poison'd Entrail to entangle more.
And so She bloats in Glory: till one Day
The Master of the House, passing that way,
Perceives, and with one flourish of his Broom
Of Web and Fly and Spider clears the Room.

'Behold, dropt through the Gate of Mortal Birth,
The Knightly Soul alights from Heav'n on Earth;
Begins his Race, but scarce the Saddle feels,   910
When a foul Imp up from the distance steals,
And, double as he will, about his Heels
Closer and ever closer circling creeps,
Then, half-invited, on the Saddle leaps,
Clings round the Rider, and, once there, in vain
The strongest strives to thrust him off again.
In Childhood just peeps up the Blade of Ill,

That Youth to Lust rears, Fury, and Self-will:
And, as Man cools to sensual Desire,
Ambition catches with as fierce a Fire;   920
Until Old Age sends him with one last Lust
Of Gold, to keep it where he found – in Dust.
Life at both ends so feeble and constrain'd
How should that Imp of Sin be slain or chain'd?

'And woe to him who feeds the hateful Beast
That of his Feeder makes an after-feast!
We know the Wolf: by Strategem and Force
Can hunt the Tiger down: but what Resource
Against the Plague we heedless hatch within,
Then, growing, pamper into full-blown Sin   930
With the Soul's self: ev'n, as the wise man said,
Feeding the very Devil with God's own Bread;
Until the Lord his Largess misapplied
Resent, and drive us wholly from his Side?

'For should the Greyhound whom a Sultan fed,
And by a jewell'd String a-hunting led,
Turned by the Way to gnaw some nasty Thing
And snarl at Him who twitch'd the silken String,
Would not his Lord soon weary of Dispute,
And turn adrift the incorrigible Brute?   940

'Nay, would one follow, and without a Chain,
The only Master truly worth the Pain,
One must beware lest, growing over-fond ⎫
Of even Life's more consecrated Bond,   ⎬
We clog our Footsteps to the World beyond. ⎭
Like that old Arab Chieftain, who confess'd
His soul by two too Darling Things possess'd –
That only Son of his: and that one Colt
Descended from the Prophet's Thunderbolt.
"And I might well bestow the last," he said,   950
"On him who brought me Word the Boy was dead."

'And if so vain the glittering Fish we get,
How doubly vain to dote upon the Net,
Call'd Life, that draws them, patching up this thin
Tissue of Breathing out and Breathing in,
And so by husbanding each wretched Thread
Spin out Death's very terror that we dread –
For as the Raindrop from the sphere of God
Dropt for a while into the Mortal Clod
So little makes of its allotted Time   960
Back to its Heav'n itself to re-sublime,
That it but serves to saturate its Clay
With Bitterness that will not pass away.'

One day the Prophet on a River Bank,
Dipping his Lips into the Channel, drank
A Draught as sweet as Honey. Then there came
One who an earthen Pitcher from the same
Drew up, and drank: and after some short stay
Under the Shadow, rose and went his Way,
Leaving his earthen Bowl. In which, anew   970
Thirsting, the Prophet from the River drew,
And drank from: but the Water that came up
Sweet from the Stream, drank bitter from the Cup.
At which the Prophet in a still Surprise
For Answer turning up to Heav'n his Eyes,
The Vessel's Earthen Lips with Answer ran –
'The Clay that I am made of once was *Man*,
Who dying, and resolved into the same
Obliterated Earth from which he came
Was for the Potter dug, and chased in turn   980
Through long Vicissitude of Bowl and Urn:
But howsoever moulded, still the Pain
Of that first mortal Anguish would retain,
And cast, and re-cast, for a Thousand years

Would turn the sweetest Water into Tears.'

———————

And after Death? – that, shirk it as we may,
Will come, and with it bring its After-Day –

For ev'n as Yusuf (when his Brotherhood
Came up from Egypt to buy Corn, and stood
Before their Brother in his lofty Place,   990
Nor knew him, for a Veil before his Face)
Struck on his Mystic Cup, which straightway then
Rung out their Story to those guilty Ten: –
Not to *them* only, but to every one;
Whatever he have said and thought and done,
Unburied with the Body shall fly up,
And gather into Heav'n's inverted Cup,
Which, stricken by God's Finger, shall tell all
The Story whereby we must stand or fall.
And though we walk this World as if behind   1000
There were no Judgement, or the Judge half-blind,
Beware, for He with whom we have to do
Outsees the Lynx, outlives the Phœnix too –

———————

So Sultan Mahmud, coming Face to Face
With mightier numbrs of the swarthy Race,
Vow'd that if God to him the battle gave,
God's Dervish People all the Spoil should have.
And God the Battle gave him; and the Fruit
Of a great Conquest coming to compute,
A Murmur through the Sultan's Army stirr'd   1010
Lest, ill committed to one hasty Word,
The Shah should squander on an idle Brood
What should be theirs who earn'd it with their Blood,

Or go to fill the Coffers of the State.
So Mahmud's Soul began to hesitate:
Till looking round in Doubt from side to side
A raving Zealot in the Press he spied,
And call'd and had him brought before his Face,
And, telling, bid him arbitrate the case.
Who, having listen'd, said – 'The Thing is plain: 1020
If Thou and God should never have again
To deal together, rob him of his share:
But if perchance you should – why then Beware!'

———

So spake the Tajidar: but Fear and Doubt
Among the Birds in Whispers went about:
Great was their Need: and Succour to be sought
At any Risk: at any Ransom bought:
But such a Monarch – greater than Mahmud
The Great Himself! Why how should he be woo'd
To listen to them? they too have come   1030
So suddenly, and unprepared from home
With any Gold, or Jewel, or rich Thing
To carry with them to so great a King –
Poor Creatures! with the old and carnal Blind,
Spite of all said, so thick upon the Mind,
Devising how they might ingratiate
Access, as to some earthly Potentate.

'Let him that with this Monarch would engage
Bring the Gold Dust of a long Pilgrimage:
The Ruby of a bleeding Heart, whose Sighs   1040
Breathe more than Amber-incense as it dies;
And while in naked Beggary he stands
Hope for the Robe of Honour from his Hands.'
And, as no gift this Sovereign receives
Save the mere Soul and Self of him who gives,

So let that Soul for other none Reward
Look than the Presence of its Sovereign Lord.'
And as his Hearers seem'd to estimate
Their Scale of Glory from Mahmud the Great,
A simple Story of the Sultan told   1050
How best a subject with his Shah made bold –

————————

One night Shah Mahmud who had been of late
Somewhat distemper'd with Affairs of State
Stroll'd through the Streets disguised, as wont to do –
And, coming to the Baths, there on the Flue
Saw the poor Fellow who the Furnace fed
Sitting beside his Water-jug and Bread.
Mahmud stept in – sat down – unask'd took up
And tasted of the untasted Loaf and Cup,
Saying within himself, 'Grudge but a bit,   1060
And, by the Lord, your Head shall pay for it!'
So having rested, warm'd and satisfied
Himself without a Word on either side,
At last the wayward Sultan rose to go.
And then at last his Host broke silence – 'So? –
Art satisfied? Well, Brother, any Day
Or Night, remember, when you come this Way
And want a bit of Provender – why, you
Are welcome, and if not – why, welcome too.' –
The Sultan was so tickled with the whim   1070
Of this quaint Entertainment and of him
Who offer'd it, that many a Night again
Stoker and Shah forgather'd in that Vein –
Till, the poor Fellow having stood the Test   ⎫
Of true Good-fellowship, Mahmud confess'd   ⎬
One Night the Sultan that had been his Guest: ⎭
And in requital of the scanty Dole
The Poor Man offer'd with so large a soul,

Bid him ask any Largess that he would –
A Throne – if he *would* have it, so he *should*.   1080
The Poor Man kiss'd the Dust, and 'All,' said he,
'I ask is what and where I am to be;
If but the Shah from time to time will come
As now and see me in the lowly Home
His presence makes a palace, and my own
Poor Flue more royal than another's Throne.'

So said the cheery Tale: and, as they heard,
Again the Heart beneath the Feather stirr'd:
Again forgot the Danger and the Woes
Of the long Travel in its glorious Close: –   1090
'Here truly all was Poverty, Despair
And miserable Banishment – but *there*
That more than Mahmud, for no more than Prayer
Who would restore them to their ancient Place,
And round their Shoulders fling his Robe of Grace.'
They clapp'd their Wings, on Fire to be assay'd
And prove of what true Metal they were made,
Although defaced, and wanting the true Ring
And Superscription of their rightful King.

'The Road! The Road!' in countless voices cried   1100
The Host – 'The Road! and who shall be our Guide?'
And they themselves 'The Tajidar!' replied:
Yet to make doubly certain that the Voice
Of Heav'n according with the People's Choice,
Lots should be drawn; and He on whom should light
Heav'n's Hand – they swore to follow him outright.
This settled, and once more the Hubbub quell'd,
Once more Suspense the Host in Silence held,
While, Tribe by Tribe, the Birds their fortune drew;
And Lo! upon the Tajidar it flew.   1110

Then rising up again in wide and high
Circumference of wings that mesh'd the sky
'The Tajidar! The Tajidar!' they cry –
'The Tajidar! The Tajidar!' with Him
Was Heav'n, and They would follow Life and Limb!
Then, once more fluttering to their Places down,
Upon his Head they set the Royal Crown
As Khalif of their Khalif so long lost,
And Captain of his now repentant Host;
And setting him on high, and Silence call'd,   1120
The Tajidar, in Pulpit-throne install'd,
His Voice into a Trumpet-tongue so clear
As all the wingéd Multitude should hear
Raised, to proclaim the Order and Array
Of March; which, many as it frighten'd – yea,
The Heart of Multitudes at outset broke,
Yet for due Preparation must be spoke.

– A Road indeed that never Wing before
Flew, nor Foot trod, nor Heart imagined – o'er
Waterless Deserts – Waters where no Shore –   1130
Valleys comprising cloud-high Mountains: these
Again their Valleys deeper than the Seas:
Whose Dust all Adders, and whose vapour Fire:
Where all once hostile Elements conspire
To set the Soul against herself, and tear
Courage to Terror – Hope into Despair,
And Madness; Terrors, Trials, to make stray
Or Stop where Death to wander or delay:
Where when half dead with Famine, Toil, and Heat,
'Twas Death indeed to rest, or drink, or eat.   1140
A Road still waxing in Self-sacrifice
As it went on: still ringing with the Cries
And Groans of Those who had not yet prevail'd,
And bleaching with the Bones of those who fail'd:
Where, almost all withstood, perhaps to earn
Nothing: and, earning, never to return. –

And first the *VALE OF SEARCH*: an endless Maze,
Branching into innumerable Ways
All courting Entrance: but one right: and this
Beset with Pitfall, Gulf, and Precipice,   1150
Where Dust is Embers, Air a fiery Sleet,
Through which with blinded Eyes and bleeding Feet
The Pilgrim stumbles, with Hyena's Howl
Around, and hissing Snake, and deadly Ghoul,
Whose Prey he falls if tempted but to droop,
Or if to wander famish'd from the Troop
For fruit that falls to ashes in the Hand,
Water that reacht recedes into the Sand.
The only word is 'Forward!' Guide in sight,
After him, swerving neither left nor right,   1160
Thyself for thine own Victual by Day,
At night thine own Self's Caravanserai.*
Till suddenly, perhaps when most subdued
And desperate, the Heart shall be renew'd
When deep in utter Darkness, by one Gleam
Of Glory from the far remote *Harím*,
That, with a scarcely conscious Shock of Change,
Shall light the Pilgrim toward the Mountain Range
Of KNOWLEDGE: where, if stronger and more pure ⎫
The Light and Air, yet harder to endure;   ⎬   1170
And if, perhaps, the Footing more secure,   ⎭
Harder to keep up with a nimble Guide,
Less from lost Road than insufficient Stride –
Yet tempted still by false Shows from the Track,
And by false Voices call'd aside or back,
Which echo from the Bosom, as if won
The Journey's End when only just begun,
And not a Mountain Peak with Toil attain'd
But shows a top yet higher to be gain'd.
Wherefore still Forward, Forward! Love that fired   1180
Thee first to search, by Search so re-inspired
As that the Spirit shall the carnal Load
Burn up, and double wing Thee on the Road;

That wert thou knocking at the very Door
Of Heav'n, thou still would'st cry for More, More, More!

Till loom in sight Kaf's Mountain Peak ashroud
In Mist – uncertain yet Mountain or Cloud,
But where the Pilgrim 'gins to hear the Tide
Of that one Sea in which the Sev'n subside;
And not the Sev'n Seas only: but the sev'n   1190
And self-enfolded Spheres of Earth and Heav'n –
Yea, the Two Worlds, that now as Pictures sleep
Upon its Surface – but when once the Deep
From its long Slumber 'gins to heave and sway – ⎫
Under the Tempest shall be swept away   ⎬
With all their Phases and Phenomena: ⎭
Not senseless Matter only, but combined
With Life in all Varieties of Kind;
Yea, ev'n the abstract Forms that Space and Time
Men call, and Weal and Woe, Virtue and Crime,   1200
And all the several Creeds like those who fell
Before them, Musulman and Infidel
Shall from the Face of Being melt away,
Cancell'd and swept as Dreams before the Day.
So hast thou seen the Astrologer prepare
His mystic Table smooth of sand, and there
Inscribe his mystic figures, Square, and Trine,
Circle and Pentagram, and heavenly Sign
Of Star and Planet: from whose Set and Rise,
Meeting and Difference, he prophesies;   1210
And, having done it, with his Finger clean
Obliterates as never they had been.

Such is when reacht the Table Land of *One*
And *Wonder*: blazing with so fierce a Sun
Of Unity that blinds while it reveals   ⎫
The Universe that to a Point congeals,   ⎬
So, stunn'd with utter Revelation, reels   ⎭

The Pilgrim, when that *Double*-seeming House,
Against whose Beams he long had chafed his Brows,
Crumbles and cracks before that Sea, whose near   1220
And nearer Voice now overwhelms his Ear.
Till blinded, deafen'd, madden'd, drunk with doubt
Of all within Himself as all without,
Nay, whether a *Without* there be, or not,
Or a *Within* that doubts: and if, then *what?* –
Ev'n so shall the bewilder'd Pilgrim seem
When nearest waking deepliest in Dream,
And darkest next to Dawn; and lost what had
When *All* is found: and just when sane quite Mad –
As one that having found the Key once more   1230
Returns, and Lo! he cannot find the Door
He stumbles over – So the Pilgrim stands
A moment on the Threshold – with raised Hands
Calls to the eternal Saki* for one Draught
Of Light from the One Essence: which when quaff'd,
He plunges headlong in: and all is well
With him who never more returns to tell.
Such being then the Race and such the Goal,
Judge if you must not Body both and Soul
With Meditation, Watch and Fast prepare.   1240
For he that wastes his body to a Hair
Shall seize the Locks of Truth: and He that prays
Good Angels in their Ministry waylays:
And the Midnightly Watcher in the Folds
Of his own Darkness God Almighty holds.
He that would prosper here must from him strip
The World, and take the Dervish Gown and Scrip:
And as he goes must gather from all Sides
Irrelevant Ambitions, Lusts and Prides,
Glory and Gold, and sensual Desire,   1250
Whereof to build the fundamental Pyre
Of Self-annihilation: and cast in
All old Relations and Regards of Kin
And Country: and, the Pile with this perplext

World platform'd, from the Fables of the Next
Raise it tow'rd Culmination, with the torn
Rags and Integuments of Creeds out-worn;
And top the giddy Summit with the Scroll ⎫
Of *Reason* that in dingy Smoke shall roll ⎬
Over the true Self-sacrifice of Soul: ⎭   1260
(For such a Prayer was his – 'O God, do Thou
With all my Wealth in the other World endow
My Friends: and with my Wealth in *this* my Foes,
Till bankrupt in *thy* Riches I repose!')
Then, all the Pile completed of the Pelf
Of either World – at last throw on *Thyself*,
And with the torch of Self-negation fire;
And ever as the Flames rise high and higher,
With Cries of agonising Glory still
All of that *Self* burn up that burn up will,   1270
Leaving the Phœnix that no Fire can slay
To spring from its own Ashes kindled – nay,
Itself an inextinguishable Spark
Of Being, *now* beneath Earth-ashes dark,
Transcending these, at last *Itself* transcends
And with the One Eternal Essence blends.

———————

The Moths had long been exiled from the Flame
They worship: so to solemn Council came,
And voted *One* of them by Lot be sent
To find their Idol. One was chosen: went.   1280
And after a long Circuit in sheer Gloom,
Seeing, he thought, the TAPER in a Room
Flew back at once to say so. But the chief
Of *Mothistan* slighted so slight Belief,
And sent another Messenger, who flew
Up to the House, in at the window, through
The Flame itself; and back the Message brings,

With yet no sign of Conflict on his wings.
Then went a Third, and spurr'd with true Desire,
Plunging at once into the sacred Fire,   1290
Folded his Wings within, till he became
One Colour and one Substance with the Flame.
He only knew the Flame who in it burn'd;
And only He could tell who ne'er to tell return'd.

After declaring what of this declared
Must be, that all who went should be prepared,
From his high Station ceased the Tajidar –
And lo! the Terrors that, when told afar,
Seem'd but as Shadows of a Noonday Sun,
Now that the talkt-of Thing was to be *done*,   1300
Lengthening into those of closing Day   ⎫
Strode into utter Darkness: and Dismay   ⎬
Like Night on the husht Sea of Feathers lay, ⎭
Late so elate – 'So terrible a Track!
Endless – or, ending, never to come back! –
Never to Country, Family, or Friend!' –
In sooth no easy Bow for Birds to bend! –
Even while he spoke, how many Wings and Crests
Had slunk away to distant Woods and Nests;
Others again in Preparation spent   1310
What little Strength they had, and never went:
And others, after preparation due –   ⎫
When up the Veil of that first Valley drew ⎬
From whose waste Wilderness of Darkness blew ⎭
A Sarsar, whether edged of Flames or Snows,
That through from Root to Tip their Feathers froze –
Up went a Multitude that overhead
A moment darken'd, then on all sides fled,
Dwindling the World-assembled Caravan
To less than half the Number that began.   1320

Of those who fled not, some in Dread and Doubt
Sat without stirring: others who set out
With frothy Force, or stupidly resign'd,
Before a League, flew off or fell behind.
And howsoever the more Brave and Strong
In Courage, Wing, or Wisdom push'd along,
Yet League by League the Road was thicklier spread
By the fast falling Foliage of the Dead:
Some spent with Travel over Wave and Ground;
Scorcht, frozen, dead for Drought, or drinking drown'd.   1330
Famisht, or poison'd with the Food when found:
By Weariness, or Hunger, or Affright
Seduced to stop or stray, become the Bite
Of Tiger howling round or hissing Snake,
Or Crocodile that eyed them from the Lake:
Or raving Mad, or in despair Self-slain:
Or slaying one another for a Grain: –

Till of the mighty Host that fledged the Dome
Of Heav'n and Floor of Earth on leaving Home,
A Handfull reach'd and scrambled up the Knees   1340
Of Kaf whose Feet dip in the Seven Seas;
And of the few that up his Forest-sides
Of Light and Darkness where *The Presence* hides,
But *Thirty* – thirty desperate draggled Things,
Half-dead, with scarce a Feather on their Wings,
Stunn'd, blinded, deafen'd with the Crash and Craze
Of Rock and Sea collapsing in a Blaze
That struck the Sun to Cinder – fell upon
The Threshold of the Everlasting *One*,
With but enough of Life in each to cry,   1350
On THAT which all absorb'd –
                          And suddenly
Forth flash'd a wingéd Harbinger of Flame
And Tongue of Fire, and 'Who?' and 'Whence they came?'
And 'Why?' demanded. And the Tajidar
For all the Thirty answer'd him – 'We are
Those Fractions of the Sum of Being, far

Dis-spent and foul disfigured, that once more
Strike for Admission at the Treasury Door.'
To whom the Angel answer'd – 'Know ye not
That He you seek recks little who or what   1360
Of Quantity and Kind – himself the Fount
Of Being Universal needs no Count
Of all the Drops o'erflowing from his Urn,
In what Degree they issue or return?'

Then cried the Spokesman, 'Be it even so:
Let us but see the Fount from which we flow,
And, seeing, lose Ourselves therein!' and, Lo!
Before the Word was utter'd, or the Tongue
Of Fire replied, or Portal open flung,
They were *within* – they were before the *Throne*,   1370
Before the Majesty that sat thereon,
But wrapt in so insufferable a Blaze
Of Glory as beat down their baffled Gaze,
Which, downward dropping, fell upon a Scroll
That, Lightning-like, flash'd back on each the whole
Past half-forgotten Story of his Soul:
Like that which Yusuf in his Glory gave
His Brethren as some Writing he would have
Interpreted; and at a Glance, behold
Their own Indenture for their Brother sold!   1380
And so with these poor Thirty: who, abasht
In Memory all laid bare and Conscience lasht,
By full Confession and Self-loathing flung
The Rags of carnal Self that round them clung;
And, their old selves self-knowledged and self-loathed,
And in the Soul's Integrity re-clothed,
Once more they ventured from the Dust to raise
Their Eyes – up to the Throne – into the Blaze,
And in the Centre of the Glory there
Beheld the Figure of – *Themselves* – as 'twere   1390
Transfigured – looking to Themselves, beheld

The Figure on the Throne en-miracled,
Until their Eyes themselves and *That* between
Did hesitate which *Sëer* was, which *Seen*;
They That, That They: Another, yet the Same:
Dividual, yet One: from whom there came
A Voice of awful Answer, scarce discern'd
From *which* to Aspiration *whose* return'd
They scarcely knew; as when some Man apart
Answers aloud the Question in his Heart –   1400
'The Sun of my Perfection is a Glass
Wherein from *Seeing* into *Being* pass
All who, reflecting as reflected see
Themselves in Me, and Me in Them: not *Me*,
But all of Me that a contracted Eye
Is comprehensive of Infinity:
Nor yet *Themselves*: no Selves, but of The All
Fractions, from which they split and whither fall.
As Water lifted from the Deep, again ⎫
Falls back in individual Drops of Rain ⎬   1410
Then melts into the Universal Main. ⎭
All you have been, and seen, and done, and thought,
Not *You* but *I*, have seen and been and wrought:
I was the Sin that from Myself rebell'd:
I the Remorse that tow'rd Myself compell'd:
I was the Tajidar who led the Track:
I was the little Briar that pull'd you back:
Sin and Contrition – Retribution owed,
And cancell'd – Pilgrim, Pilgrimage, and Road,
Was but Myself toward Myself: and Your   1420
Arrival but *Myself* at my own Door:
Who in your Fraction of Myself behold
Myself within the Mirror Myself hold
To see Myself in, and each part of Me
That sees himself, though drown'd, shall ever see.
Come you lost Atoms to your Centre draw,
And *be* the Eternal Mirror that you saw:

Rays that have wander'd into Darkness wide
Return, and back into your Sun subside.' –

———————

This was the Parliament of Birds: and this   1430
The Story of the Host who went amiss,
And of the Few that better Upshot found;
Which being now recounted, Lo, the Ground
Of Speech fails underfoot: But this to tell –
Their Road is thine – Follow – and Fare thee well.   1435

———————

Notes

The Rubaiyat of Omar Khayyam

All 105 quatrains of the present edition are listed below, each with an indication of its provenance. The first number in parentheses indicates the edition, the second indicates the stanza number; thus (five: 74) denotes the seventy-fourth stanza of the fifth edition.

Stanza

1 (one:1)   **The Stone that puts the Stars to Flight?**   a stone flung into a cup was a call to depart.

2 (one:2)   **Dawn's Left Hand:**   early light just before the dawn.

3 (one:3)

4 (one:4)   WHITE HAND OF MOSES: blossoms in spring. (See Exodus 4.6.) **suspires:**   the healing power of Jesus was said to reside in his breath.

5 (one:5)   **Iram:**   an ancient garden-city of legend. **Jamshyd:** legendary king of old Persia, founder of Persepolis. His **seven-ringed cup** depicted the seven divisions of the globe.

6 (one:6)   **Pehlevi** (also Pahlavi):   Middle Persian, as spoken and written from the third to the ninth century AD.

7 (one:7)

8 (five:8)   **Naishapur:**   birthplace and home town of Omar Khayyam.

9 (one:8)   **Kaikobad:**   legendary Persian king.

10 (one:9)   **Kaikhosru:**   legendary Persian king.
   Rustum: legendary Persian hero, equivalent to Hercules.
   Hatim Tai: an Arab chieftain celebrated as a man of extravagant hospitality.

11 (one:10)   **Mahmud:**   Sultan Mahmud of Ghazna (ruled 998–1030), celebrated as a great conqueror who extended the territory of Persia.

12 (five:12)

13 (one:12)

14 (one:13)

15 (one:14)

16 (one:15)

17 (two:14)   **Spider-like:**   This striking metaphor probably belongs not to Omar Khayyam but to Attar. It is more fully developed in a sonnet-like sequence in *Bird Parliament*. See lines 894–907. Lines 3–4 of this stanza strongly recall lines 954–55 of *Bird Parliament*.

18 (one:16)   **Caravanserai:**   an inn, sometimes taken as a symbol of the transience of human life.

19 (one:17)   **Bahram:**   a great hunter of Persian legend, equivalent to Nimrod. (See Genesis 10.9.)

20 (one:18)

21 (one:19)

22 (two:20)   Another borrowing from Attar. The cooing Ringdove appears in *Bird Parliament*, lines 505–18. This stanza is sometimes published without the second 'and' in line 4; that word is needed for proper scansion.

23 (one:20)

24 (one:21)

25 (one:22)

26 (one:23)

27 (five:25)   **Muezzin:**   Muslim official whose duty is to call the faithful to prayer.

28 (one:25)

29 (two:77)

30 (one:26)

31 (one:27)

32 (one:28)

33 (one:29)

34 (one:30)

35 (one:31)

36 (one:32)

37 (one:33)

38 (five:33)

39 (five:35)

40 (one:35)

41 (one:36)

42 (five:38)

43 (one:37)

44 (five:39)

45 (five:40)

46 (five:41)

47 (one:47)

48 (one:48)

49 (five:44)

50 (five:45)   **Ferrash:**   servant.

51 (five:46)   **Saki:**   cupbearer.

52 (five:47)

53 (one:38)

54 (five:49)

55 (five:50)   **Alif:**   the first letter of the Arabic alphabet, a vertical line.

56 (five:51)   **Mah:**   moon. **Mahi:**   fish. See *Bird Parliament*, line 45, and note.

57 (five:52)

58 (five:53)

59 (one:39)

60 (five:55)

61 (five:56)

62 (five:57)   This stanza is a modest self-reference. In the Islamic world Omar Khayyam's greatest claim to fame is that he headed a commission that reformed the calendar with remarkable accuracy.

63 (one:42)

64 (one:43)

65 (one:44)

66 (one:45)

67 (five:61)

68 (five:62)

69 (five:64)

70 (five:65)

71 (five:66)

72 (five:67)

73 (one:46)

74 (one:49)

75 (one:50)   **The Ball:**   This and other sporting references in this stanza appear to refer to Polo, which is of oriental origin. Cf. *Bird of Parliament* lines 851–3.

76 (one:51)

77 (one:52)

78 (one:53)

79 (five:74)

80 (one:54)   **Parwin:**   the star cluster known as The Pleiades.
Mushtara: the planet Jupiter.

81 (one:55)   **Sufi:**   Islamic mystic.

82 (five:77)

83 (five:78)

84 (five:79)

85 (one:57)

86 (one:58)

87 (one:59)   **Kuza-Nama:**   This heading appeared only in the First Edition.
Ramazan: (Ramadan) the ninth month of the Muslim calendar, a period of dawn-to-dusk fasting.

88 (one:60)

89 (one:61)

90 (one:62)

91 (one:63)

92 (one:64)

93 (one:65)

94 (one:66)   **Crescent:**   the first glimpse of the new moon, marking the end of Ramadan.

95 (one:67)

96 (one:68)

97 (one:69)

98 (one:70)

99 (one:71)

100 (one:72)

101 (five:97)

102 (five:98)

103 (one:73)

104 (one:74)

105 (one:75) **Made one:** means 'died'.

Bird Parliament

FitzGerald's notes are marked [EFG].

Line

10 **Khalif:** title given to an Islamic spiritual leader regarded as a successor of Mohammed. (Also Calif, Caliph).

33 **Tajidar:** '*Crown-wearer*' – one Epithet of the '*Hudhud*', a beautiful kind of Lapwing, Niebuhr says, frequenting the Shores of the Persian Gulf, and supposed to have the Gift of Speech, etc. [EFG].

45 **From Cloud to Fish:** From Màh, the Moon, to Màhi, the Fish, on which the World was fabled to repose [EFG].

47 **Sulayman:** Solomon.

74 **Symurgh:** i.e. 'Thirty-Birds' – a fabulous Creature like the Griffin of our Middle Ages: the Arabian *Anka* [EFG]. This name amounts to a spiritual and linguistic pun, whereby *Si morg* (thirty birds) aspire towards, and then themselves become, *Semorgh* (God).

151   **Shah Mahmud:**   see *Rubaiyat*, note on stanza 11.

160   **Salam:**   a word and gesture of greeting in Muslim society, (also *salaam*).

163   **Amir:**   title of some Muslim princes.

215   **The Notes of Him whose Life is lost in hers:**   It was sometimes fancied that the Rose had as many Petals as her Lover had Notes in his Voice [EFG].

227   **As David's Finger Iron did of old:**   The Prophet David was supposed, in Oriental Legend, to have had the power to mould Iron into a Cuirass with the miraculous Power of his Finger [EFG].

257   **Who else with him:**   Khizar, Prophet and Keeper of the Well of Life; habited always in the Green which the angels were supposed to wear; and, whether from that reason, or some peculiar Phenomenon in the air, constantly called Sky-colour by the Persian Poets [EFG].

274   **Heav'n's Woof entire:**   The Sky is constantly called *Green* in Persian Poetry: whether because of the Tree of Heaven *Sidra*: or of some fabled Emerald in Kaf on which the World hinges: or because Green has been chosen (for whatever Reason) for the Colour of *Life* and Honour. The green tinge of some Oriental Skies is indeed noticed by Travellers: as we see a little also in our Northern Sunrise and Sunset: but still it must be an exceptional Phenomenon. *Blue*, or *Purple*, is rather devoted to Death and Mourning in the East. As, in this very Poem, one of the Stories is of the Sea being askt 'why he dresses his Waves in Blue?' – And he answers he does so for the Loss of *One* who never will return [EFG].

300   **that Sev'n-headed Snake:**   And, as the tradition went, let the Snake into Eden [EFG].

327   **Sarsar of the North:** a cold Blast [EFG].

429   **an Apple on my Head:**   Tell's Apple, long before his Time: and, by whomsoever invented, a Fancy which (as was likely) would take lasting hold of the Oriental Mind. In Chodzko's *Popular Persian Songs*

(Oriental Translation Fund, 1842) is a sort of Funeral Chaunt on Zulfakhar Khan by one of his Slaves; and the following Passage in it: 'Your Gun from the Manufactory of Loristan shines like a Cloud gilded by the Rays of the Sun. O Serdar! your Place is now empty: you were my Master: Your Gun from the Manufactory of Cabul shined in your Hands like a Bunch of Roses. Your Ball never missed a Flower put in the middle of my Front Hair' [EFG].

437   **as gave the Crown:**   He was supposed to be destined to Sovereignty over whom the Shadow of the wings of the Phoenix passed [EFG].

506   **Yúsuf:**   Joseph.

523–4   **the Bird of Heav'n:**   Gabriel [EFG].

706   **Sidra:**   the Tree of Paradise, or Heaven [EFG].

767   **Munkar and wakyr:**   The two Angels who examine the Soul on its leaving the Body [EFG].

851   **Maidan:**   an open space used for sports.

853   **the World's Game:**   see note on *Rubaiyat*, stanza 75.

892   **Nembroth:**   Nimrod [EFG].

897   **The Spider:**   cf. note on *Rubaiyat*, stanza 17.

1162   **Caravanserai:**   see note on *Rubaiyat*, stanza 18.

1234   **Saki:**   cupbearer.

1294   This line is a metrical irregularity, a single hexameter among regular pentameters. It reads very well as such, drawing out its sense at greater length in a way that suits its terminal position and acquiring emphasis in the process. It is not known whether this is a deliberate interpolation by FitzGerald or a happy mistake.

Guide to Further Reading

Bloom, Harold, editor, *Edward FitzGerald's 'The Rubaiyat of Omar Khayyam'*. Bloom's Modern Critical Interpretations, Chelsea House, Philadelphia, USA, 252pp., 2004. 0–7910–7538–4.

Briggs, A. D. P., *Edward FitzGerald*, Literary Encyclopedia, www.litencyc.com.

Brodie, Richard, *The Rubaiyat of Omar Khayyam. A Complete Online Resource*, www.therubaiyat.com/brodie.

Drabble, Margaret, editor, *The Oxford Companion to English Literature*, 6th edition, Oxford University Press, Oxford, 2000.

Garrard, Garry, *A Book of Verse: The Biography of the 'Rubaiyat of Omar Khayyam'*, Sutton Publishing, Stroud, 270pp., 2007. Hardback 978–0–7509–4631–5. Paperback 978–0–7509–4632–2.

Martin, William H. and Sandra Mason, *The Art of Omar Khayyam: Illustrating FitzGerald's 'Rubaiyat'*, I. B. Tauris, London, 184pp., 2007. 978–1–84511–282–0.

Ousby, Ian, editor, *The Cambridge Guide to English Literature*, Cambridge University Press, Cambridge, 1988.

Potter, A. G., *A Bibliography of the Rubaiyat of Omar Khayyam* (Ingpen and Grant, London, 1929), reissued by Georg Olms Verlag, Hildersheim, 1994.

Wilton, Andrew and Robert Upstone, editors, *The Age of*

Rossetti, Burne-Jones & Watts. Symbolism in Britain 1860–1910, Tate Gallery Publishing, London, 1997.

A splendid colour print showing the cover of *'The Great Omar'* ('one of the finest examples of the bookbinder's craft'), which went down with the *Titanic* in 1912, is available from Shepherd's Bookbinders, 76 Rochester Row, London SW1P 1JU. The story is told in Rob Shepherd, *Lost on the Titanic*, Shepherds, Sangorski & Sutcliffe and Zaensdorf, London, 2001.